1972

Faith from the Abyss

Hermann Hesse's Way
from Romanticism to Modernity

by ERNST ROSE

NEW YORK UNIVERSITY PRESS 1965

PREFACE

ANYONE writing about Hermann Hesse today no longer can start at the beginning. But to assert that I have read all Hesse criticism would be just as arrogant as to deny the debt I owe to some of its faithful practitioners. Those studies that proved especially helpful and those that appeared to me to be basic for an understanding of Hesse are listed in the appendix.

Quotations from Hesse's works have been given in English translation, to retain the stylistic unity of the book. The translations are my own, although I have freely used the existing English versions by Hilda Rosner (*Siddhartha*), Josef Mileck and Horst Frenz (*Steppenwolf*), and Merwyn Savell (*Magister Ludi*), which are generally excellent. Permission to quote numerous passages from Hesse's works in translation was graciously and generously granted by Suhrkamp Verlag, Frankfurt am Main, the exclusive owners of the copyright.

A special expression of gratitude goes to my good friend Prof. Robert Clements of New York University, associate editor of the Gotham Library. Without his encouragement this book would not even have been started. My esteemed colleague, Prof. Dorothea Berger, and my dear wife, Hildegard Rose, read the first draft of the manuscript and suggested numerous improvements. Mrs. Ellen MacKenzie did a very conscientious job in editing the copy for the printer, and Mrs. Doris Starr Guilloton of Washington Square College helped very generously with the proofreading and the index. I am also grateful to the students of my undergraduate Hesse course, who by

v

their intelligent questions and discussions enriched my thinking
in many ways. Last but not least, I received much inspiration from three of our Ph.D. candidates who by their disserta-
tions and correspondence contributed greatly to the gestation
of this book: Emanuel Meyer, Gisela Stein of Brooklyn College,
and Fred H. Willecke of Wagner College.

E.R.

CONTENTS

Faith from the Abyss

MOTTO

Man can escape his self-inflicted predicament and solve the social, political, and cultural problems of the present age only by realizing his intrinsic destiny to live in truth. He cannot find the fulfillment of his destiny in obedience to the slogans of others, or in joining some organization. He can only find it by realizing his own, special responsibility.

—Karl Jaspers

Introduction

OF ALL the roads of access to the proper understanding of a writer that of the literary critic seems to be the most natural one. Our first attention is after all aroused by the writer's published works, and we should never be interested in the details of his personal life independent of their relation to those works. Literary biography, unless it is approached primarily with a psychological or sociological interest, will for the aesthetic reader always remain a subsidiary occupation. Being little concerned with it, he will in any case avoid the pitfalls of confusing the author with his characters, of taking his middlemen and his spokesmen for the writer himself. A nonbiographical approach will make us appreciate literature as literature, as a separate entity following its own aesthetic laws. Great literature has never really "copied" or "imitated" life.

Neither has literature ever existed in a vacuum. It is produced by living persons and is enjoyed by readers in the flesh. It grows out of the quandaries of human and artistic existence and somehow reflects them. As surely as there are cases where the reflection is oblique or indirect, so are there others where the connection between art and life appears to be close and almost undisrupted. This second case we have before us in the works of Hermann Hesse. So much from his own personal background and from his adolescent and childhood experiences has entered into his writings that for long stretches they read almost like a spiritual autobiography.

It therefore seemed proper to approach Hesse first from

a biographical perspective. In the case of young Hesse, the naive reader will always be tempted to use that approach. Later, to be sure, the autobiographical character of Hesse's works becomes open to suspicion, and a clear distinction between actual autobiography and essential fiction is warranted. But the distinction already exists in the early works, although to a less obvious degree, and the critical biographer will be obliged to point this out.

In any case, biographical curiosity in this particular case seems justified, and we will endeavor to satisfy it as much as Hesse's work seems to demand it. Our narrative will clear up many otherwise obscure allusions and will prove beyond cavil the reality of the existential problem raised in Hesse's written works. But we also hope to make the reader aware at the outset of the essentially aesthetic context in which this problem is raised, and of the essentially artistic logic which prompted Hesse to make use of his personal experiences and reminiscences. We are aiming at a full portrait of a great writer. The discriminating reader, therefore, should not be troubled by biographical data which at first must seem inconsequential, but will later prove to have entered the writer's works in valid artistic disguise.

1 · Childhood and Youth *

WHEN HERMANN HESSE was born in 1877, the German Empire was six years old. Wilhelm I was still emperor, and Otto von Bismarck would continue as chancellor for many years to come. German prosperity, which had been spurred by the victorious Franco-Prussian War, was reaching new heights, and the age of German importance in world politics was dawning. Machinery was rapidly replacing hand crafts; and the telephone, the telegraph, and the railroad were enabling men and ideas to move swiftly to new areas. Bourgeois moral standards, however, held firm; Christianity was the ruling convention; and the dominant roles of the father and the teacher were taken for granted by most Germans.

Yet the army of industrial workers was multiplying daily, the cities were expanding, and the population curve was soaring. It would seem, therefore, that the world of bourgeois prosperity was less secure than it seemed. Karl Marx had published his *Communist Manifesto* twenty-nine years before Hesse's birth. Sigmund Freud was a twenty-one year old university student. The first part of Friedrich Nietzsche's *Thoughts out of Season* had appeared four years earlier; his *Zarathustra* came six years later. Twenty-four years after Hesse's birth, Thomas Mann's *Buddenbrooks* would detail the decline and downfall of bour-

* The numbers refer by volume and page to the final German edition of Hesse's collected writings, *Gesammelte Schriften* (Vols. I–VII. Berlin: Suhrkamp, 1957). The transalations are the author's own. Years indicate dates of first publication, whether in magazine or book form.

3

geois civilization, and Albert Einstein would be finishing his studies at the Zurich Graduate School of Technology. Most notably, thirty-seven years later the outbreak of World War I would mark the end of German prosperity, of German world politics, of the monarchical form of government, and postwar developments would demonstrate the bankruptcy of private and political morals.

To a sensitive mind, then, this was an age of contrasts and of profound change. To be born into it gave an individual feelings of insecurity and challenged him to seek new paths to contentment; to look for new values to offset questionable traditions. The way might be made smoother or more difficult if the searcher was an outsider not wholly attuned to the German style of living. In Hesse's case this was the problem. His family did not come from the mainstream of German cultural life, and its spiritual foundations reached into non-European worlds of thinking.

Hesse's paternal grandfather, Dr. Carl Hermann Hesse, was of Russian-German lineage. He was a county physician and state councillor in the Estonian city of Weissenstein, a practical and jovial character in spite of his ingrained Pietism. Already he was deeply involved in Christian missionary work, and many missionaries to India came as guests to his home. Their stories left an indelible impression on the receptive mind of his son Johannes. The boy, who was born to Carl's first wife, Jenny Lass, in 1847, lost his mother when he was four. Doctor Hesse's second wife died in childbirth, and his third wife, Adele von Berg, raised Johannes.

Johannes, after completing his early studies in local schools, was a pupil at the renowned Cathedral School of Reval (now Tallinn). When he was old enough to decide what he wanted to do with his life, he chose the career of a missionary, even though he had been, in typical pietist fashion, beset for a long time by doubts about his "worthiness."

At the age of seventeen, Johannes moved to Basel to receive formal instruction in the house of the famous Basel Mission Society. He devoted three years to Bible and language study and one year to secretarial training in the office of the society's inspector; he also became a Swiss citizen. Then the mission committee, after due deliberation, sent Johannes Hesse to India. Taking leave of his parents in Estonia, Hesse went there in the fall of 1869 and became an assistant to a missionary in the Blue Mountains. He learned the Badaga and Kanarese languages, and everything seemed to be going well, when Johannes became ill. A Scottish general named Mackenzie nursed him back to health and then accompanied him to Europe when it became evident that the young missionary could not endure the tropical climate.

Johannes paid a brief visit to his parents at Weissenstein before he was called to Calw, a city on the Nagold River in the grand duchy of Württemberg. Here he met Dr. Hermann Gundert, who had moved there after decades of Indian missionary work. The doctor was the director of the Calw Publishing House of the Basel Mission Society which published mission magazines and was preparing a definitive dictionary of the Malayalam tongue. Naturally Dr. Gundert was glad to acquire an enthusiastic young assistant.

Dr. Gundert and his wife Julia, a fiery Swiss Calvinist from the Dubois family of Neuchâtel vintagers, had a daughter Marie. The young woman, who had married a missionary named Isenberg and bore him three sons, was living with her parents following the death of her husband in India. Johannes met her at the Gunderts' home. They became engaged in the summer of 1874 and were married in November of the same year.

Marie bore her second husband six children, two of whom died in infancy. She later suffered from a kidney disease, to which she succumbed in 1902. At the time of her death, her son Hermann was 29 years old and had barely taken the first steps on the ladder to literary fame.

After Marie's death, Johannes Hesse led a lonely existence aggravated by headaches and frequent neuralgic pains. He became increasingly discontented with life in the small provincial town with its gossip and its dogmatic views of Christianity. Finally his eyesight was affected and he became blind. Still, his spirit refused to surrender, and he continued to write books on religious problems. One of them was *Lao-tse, a Pre-Christian Witness of Truth.* Johannes died in a secluded pietist colony on March 8, 1916. On his gravestone appears a verse from the

Psalms which he himself had selected: "The rope is torn, the bird is free."

Hermann Hesse, born at Calw on July 2, 1877, was the second child of Marie and Johannes. Of his other brothers and sisters only Adele deserves particular mention. She was older than Hermann, and to the end of her days remained on affectionate terms with her brother. The two eventually collaborated in the writing of their father's biography.

Hermann Hesse grew up in a decidedly pietistic atmosphere. Although, historically speaking, Pietism had started in the late seventeenth century as a movement for the revival of the Lutheran Church, it was actually a renewal of mystic tendencies which since the Middle Ages had formed an important phase of the Christian religion. It had first been systematically explored by Meister Eckhart and other Dominican monks of the fourteenth century. Like mysticism in general, Pietism was by no means a purely German affair. It had its counterparts in other West European countries under such names as Methodism and Jansenism. Its concern with missionary work also predisposed it toward a deeper understanding of non-Christian religious experience and it had become colored, to some extent, with non-Christian mysticism.

Pietism, which even today has remained a potent, spiritual force, thoroughly imbued nineteenth-century Swabian culture. It spawned whole literary and artistic, philosophical, and even political movements. Leading German poets and philosophers had grown up under its influence.

In Hermann Hesse's family, Pietism pervaded all daily activities and provided the guiding principles in the education of the children. For Hermann's father, man's salvation through the death of Jesus Christ was the beginning and the end of all belief. But salvation was a wholly personal affair. There were no dogmatically fixed rules for Christianity. Everything must be held in flux so that the right spirit could enter into all decisions.

From Pietism young Hesse received the impulse toward the painstaking search of his conscience and the critical analysis of all his motives which found expression in so much of his work. But at the same time pietistic inwardness brought him into conflict with accepted worldly standards. Beyond the confines of his father's study lay the fairy-tale world of his mother, the learned and literary world of Gundert's grandfather with its treasure of eighteenth-century novels and Indian legends, the bountiful Swabian countryside with its many sounds and colors. The conflict between the world and the spirit pervaded all of Hermann Hesse's early life. Although later he sought to solve it in various ways, he never met with complete success and with subtle or even grim irony described his life as a failure to his last years.

Until the end of Hesse's life, his father remained an inspiring example of living faith. The poet spoke admiringly of the "royal poverty" of his parents, "their openhandedness toward poverty, their brotherliness toward fellow Christians, their concern for the heathen, the whole enthused heroism of their Christian life" (VII, 372). Once he summarized the importance of his parental home in confessing that "Christianity, not preached but practised, has been the strongest among the powers which have educated me and have formed me" (VII, 744-745).

At the same time, however, young Hesse sensed the gap between his father's practices and his beliefs. At times he almost hated his father's terminology and believed it to be thoroughly out of date. In later years he was more inclined to admit that his father, too, was dissatisfied with the positions taken by contemporary theology, but could not quite shake them off. There were, on the one hand, the lofty ideals of historical Protestantism, and on the other, the equally high purpose of finding a more lasting and contemporary formulation of Christian faith. Yet each word had a limited meaning, and everywhere regional churches and pious brotherhoods were fighting for their own interpretations instead of joining in a harmonious community of Christian faith.

It was characteristic of Johannes that he discovered Lao-tse and was deeply moved by him. Yet though this was a step beyond Luther and the pietist Count Zinzendorf, it was not a step beyond Christianity. Hermann Hesse believed that even in his most audacious intellectual sallies, his father remained within the Christian fold. If he had ever gone beyond it, Johannes would have felt that something was lost forever. But at least he struggled with the problem, and the son's strong aversion to orthodoxy and institutionalized religion had its last roots in the father's pietist conviction of the relativity of dogmatic fixations.

The father's educational methods unfortunately did not correspond to the high spirit of his principles. Education for him meant the submission of the child to the parent and aimed at the breaking of his individual will. But young Hermann was neither meek nor submissive and was determined not to be broken. After all, the father's world of strict responsibility was not the only one. There was also the peaceful sphere of the mother. Rich in imagination, alive with colorful lore, it projected its sympathies and anticipated one's needs. "The mother or sister came, one was served tea and felt himself surrounded by loving care, and one could weep or sleep, in order to awake afterwards healthy and happy in a completely changed, saved, and bright world" (III, 436). It was between this warm sphere of the mother and the stern realm of the father that the soul of young Hesse was divided. Here the inner schism, which forms the theme of most of his later novels, had its roots.

Instinctively, Hermann turned to nature where the conflicts of the home did not exist. In a touching letter to his sister Adele after the end of World War II, Hesse reminded her of the many summer Sunday forenoons when they wandered through rye and wheat fields ablaze with blue corn flowers and red poppies, over dry stretches of heath sprouting silver thistles and high-stalked gentian. He reminisced about their mother's little garden with its blossoms of bleeding heart and phlox and about cold Easter mornings when they set out to search for the Easter eggs hidden under the trees. Beautiful also

was the September sun on those high festival days of our childhood when we ate plum cake under the old chestnut trees and the boys shot at the wooden eagle. . . . Beautiful were the hidden paths in the tall fir forest, with the ferns and the high red-blooming foxglove, and our father at times stopped at a white fir tree, scratched a resin bubble with his pocket knife and let a clear drop of resin fall into a little flask. He preserved it, in order perhaps to spread it on occasion over a small wound, or only to smell it (VII, 444).

But soon again the old town of Calw with the family's ancient house would claim his attention. Hesse has subsequently described his home town in *The Cyclone* (*Der Zyklon*, 1913;

I, 762–780)—the historical half-timbered houses with their
pointed gables, the cobblestone streets and alleys, the narrow
bridge over the Nagold River, and the church steeple in the
center of the town. From its upper gallery on Sundays the town
musicians sounded forth a hymn, the text of which might have
been written by Paul Gerhardt or the saintly Gerhard Terstee-
gen. The melody was often composed by Johann Sebastian Bach
and was just as familiar.

The house in which Hermann Hesse was born was built on
a hillside, so that the back of the uppermost floor was level with
the ground. From it one stepped into a small garden. The façade,
on the other hand, had many floors. Like all old-fashioned German houses, it boasted of a *gute Stube*, a parlor occupied only
on festive occasions. Here stood the Christmas tree next to the
miniature manger and its surroundings. Here also was a place
for the piano, next to the music stand with the church hymns,
the profane songs of Friedrich Silcher and Franz Schubert, and
the piano scores of the great Protestant oratorios. Such music
occupied an important place throughout Hesse's life. He early
learned to play the violin as well as the flute.

The house also held other attractions. The roomy corridor
had a red sandstone tile floor. It contained a wardrobe crowned
by a bust of Dr. Gotthilf Heinrich von Schubert, the family
friend and romantic author of *The Symbolism of Dreams* and
of *The History of the Soul*. Next to it was the grandfather's
library with its thousands of books of all centuries and of many
countries, among which young Hermann could browse to his
heart's content. It contained not only learned works on theology
and oriental philology, but also translations of the sacred books
of the East and a goodly number of eighteenth-century novels
and Romantic writings. It was here that Hesse first made the
acquaintance of the novels of Christian Fürchtegott Gellert,
Johann Gottfried Schnabel, and Jean Paul, and of the poetry
of Novalis. At Easter there were eggs dyed in home-made vege-
table colors, the most beautiful of which were decorated with
tiny painted flowers, grass blossoms, or dwarf ferns on a yellow
background. When the weather was unfriendly, they were
hidden in the corridor or behind the books.

The entire house exuded the spirit of grandfather Gundert,

who was a most learned philologist, at home not only in Sanskrit but also in many Indian dialects. Amid the tobacco clouds of his study one could discern the figures of Indian gods, and the wardrobes of grandmother Gundert contained Indian rosaries of wooden beads, palm leaf scrolls with scratched-in holy texts, carved jade turtles, and fine Bengal weavings. When the children were small, they were over-awed by their grandfather, who could sing songs of the Kanarese and the Singhalese, songs from Bengal and Hindustan, who knew the prayer rites of the Mohammedans and the Buddhists, although he was a Christian and believed in the Holy Trinity.

In his early teens Hermann actually harbored some fear of his grandfather. But this fear vanished on a fateful day when the lad ran away from the Maulbronn monastery school and returned home. He climbed the stairs to his grandfather's study with a heavy heart, ready to submit to his judgment, and timidly opened the door. But the bearded patriarch merely looked with friendly sympathy into the frightened face of his grandson, and said: "They tell me, Hermann, that you have made a little academic side-trip" (ein Genie-Reisle) (VII, 442). No reproaches or scoldings followed.

The old man was a true sage, knowing and therefore tolerating the ways of the world, full of kindness and helpfulness that at times bordered on the magic. He was venerated and loved by the many visitors who came into contact with him.

Hermann Hesse early became acquainted with the brown faces of Indian scholars and the sallow complexions of English missionaries. He heard his grandfather converse in English, French, Italian, and East Indian and Malayan dialects. The atmosphere of the house was truly international. Hermann's father had renounced his Russian citizenship when he had moved to Basel. The oldest of Hermann's step-brothers had been born in India and was a British subject. The second oldest was naturalized in Württemberg, where he went to study. The rest of the children were Swiss citizens like their father during their years in elementary school. Grandmother Gundert spoke no German and read a French Bible. Even Hermann's own mother had been in India for a long time, and she too spoke and sang Malayalam and Kanarese, and exchanged with her aged father words and sayings in strange, magic tongues. Here, in this home so uncommon in provincial Swabia, "every soul, and especially every Christian soul, weighed equally, and neither Jew nor Negro, neither Hindu nor Chinese was a stranger or was excluded" (VII, 439).

To be sure, this world was also outspokenly German and Protestant. It was also the world of Matthias Claudius and Joseph von Eichendorff; of the Swabian God-seekers Johann Albrecht Bengel and Friedrich Oetinger, Christian Gottlieb Barth, and the famous faith healer Johann Christoph Blumhardt, with whom the family had maintained close and friendly relations. It was also the world of humanistic Latin and Greek erudition. But it was a world that was never lacking in an awareness of the whole colorful life outside the European and Christian sphere. Though in some ways it might appear anachronistic in an age of technical civilization and of fierce international rivalries, in other respects it was far advanced beyond the narrow nationalisms beclouding the view of most of Hesse's contemporaries, and already anticipated a future of peaceful international cooperation and truly human culture.

To be sure, young Hesse's world was not without contradictions, and its well-arranged orderliness was deceptive. But for the children it was primarily a rich and colorful world, stimulating and often exciting, and they saw no incongruity in this jumble of forest and river, of fox and doe, neighbors and aunts, Christmas and Easter, Latin and Greek, Jean Paul and the *Mahabharata*. It was their own world, which belonged to them as did the sunshine and the rain.

Yet the peace and harmony embracing them could not last forever. In the spring of 1881 the Hesse family moved to Basel, and it was here that young Hermann first asserted his independence of spirit by an occasional truancy. When his father was called to Calw in 1886 to take over the direction of the Mission Publishing House from Dr. Gundert, the family home had to be exchanged for larger quarters.

Then in 1890 Hermann was sent for a year to the town of Göppingen to prepare for his college entrance examination. His early teachers had left him indifferent to study, but perhaps that was for the best, as it gave Hesse's mind freedom to rove at will.

He scribbled his first verses in his notebooks and discovered for himself the alluring lilt of Friedrich Hölderlin's subtle poetry. Now at Göppingen he came under the supervision of the famous rector Otto Bauer, a quizzical scholar of the old school, who knew how to challenge his pupils by setting up the highest goals for them, and who yet had remained child enough to take part in their fun and games.

Hesse blossomed under his tutelage and in July 1891 passed the entrance examination to the Maulbronn seminary. (Maulbronn was an old monastery that had been converted to a Protestant boarding school and was one of the mainstays of the Swabian classical tradition.) Hermann had had to change his Swiss citizenship to that of Württemberg in order to be admitted. Life and study at Maulbronn, which were later reflected in the Mariabronn episodes of *Narcissus and Goldmund*, at first proved exhilarating. Homer and Ovid, Friedrich Schiller and Friedrich Klopstock, attracted the young mind. The ancient Gothic building and the congenial society of equally high-minded fellow students uplifted his spirit.

Yet suddenly and apparently without any particular provocation, Hesse ran away from school on a cold February day. He slept in an open field and returned the next day only when brought back by a state trooper. Punishment by solitary confinement could not be avoided, but it meant little hardship. It was only a few days later that he could give an account of what had happened. The Maulbronn school, to be sure, was nice enough, but even the nicest school represented confinement and offended his sensibilities. After a second brief try he gave up Maulbronn altogether.

An inner crisis developed, in which a highly excitable and nervous young mind fought for assertion against a world which had suddenly lost all meaning and had thrown him into the deepest of depressions. He even attempted suicide. The worried parents sent their problem son first to the faith healer Christoph Blumhardt, whose father was Johann Christoph Blumhardt (famous for faith healing), then to an institution for mentally retarded children.

A later sojourn at a Cannstatt *Gymnasium* yielded Hesse a certificate for voluntary military service (*Einjährig-Freiwilligen*

Zeugnis), but soon again the youth was spending many evenings in the taverns and going into debt. He remained volatile and unstable and was obviously unfit for a theological or teaching career. Hesse's father then encouraged him to learn the book trade, but the apprenticeship lasted only three days. Next, the father decided to enroll Hermann as a mechanic, and from June 1894 to September 1895 he became a metal-worker in Master Heinrich Perrot's Calw clock shop.

These months spent at the vise and the lathe with file and hacksaw and soldering iron, had the desired salutary effect. Hesse came to a realization of his mission. He would be a writer. From the time he had learned how to write he had made verses. Among other items from his youth, a fairy tale has been preserved which Hesse wrote at the age of ten as a birthday present for his younger sister Marulla (IV, 928–936). Now, seven or eight years later, he had become aware that he was born to be a writer and a poet and he took the necessary steps to prepare for such a career. Systematically and voraciously he oriented himself in the best existing literature. He read Goethe and the German Romantic writers, Dickens and Sterne, Swift and Fielding, Cervantes and Grimmelshausen, Ibsen and Zola. He gained decisive motivation from Vladimir Korolenko. And he wrote nostalgic verse in the traditional romantic style of Eichendorff and Emanuel Geibel.

Hermann had found himself and was now willing to face the challenge of everyday life. He acceded to the advice of his parents and became an apprentice in the Heckenhauer bookshop at Tübingen.

2 · In the Wake of Romanticism

THE TÜBINGEN BOOKSHOP which Hesse entered in October 1895 was an old-fashioned establishment. The apprentice had to spend from ten to twelve hours daily at the standing-desk or behind the counter, and he was by no means spared the tasks of wrapping packages and addressing catalogues. When he came home to his furnished room in the evening, he was exhausted. But the new activity was interesting and it also offered meager financial rewards. Hesse decorated his room with the portraits of writers, artists, and other famous men. The photographs of Nietzsche and of Gerhart Hauptmann were bought with Hesse's own meager funds. But this pin-up collection was only the visible expression of the independent life of the mind which the young man now created for himself after hours.

He soon rejected the last traces of an affected atheism and materialism and returned to the spiritual orientation of his childhood, though not to orthodox Christianity. Moses Mendelssohn's *Phaidon* and the poetic chapters of the Old Testament especially corroborated Hermann's new creed. Still he was not willing to lose himself in isolated spiritual contemplation and did not withdraw entirely from old and new student friends in this university town where a bookseller was not excluded from academic life. Yet the time dedicated to conviviality was limited, since most of his free hours were of necessity devoted to study.

He concentrated on Goethe, whose *Reineke Fuchs, Wilhelm Meister's Apprenticeship,* and *Truth and Poetry* inspired

14

Hesse with their harmonious outlook on life. Characteristically, he avoided the problematic approach of *Faust*. Other classical writers like Schiller and Gotthold Lessing, Vergil and Homer, proved equally stimulating. And the German Romantic poets captivated Hesse, especially Novalis, of whose writings he read every word. To Novalis he dedicated one of his early stories, and the poet became Hesse's guiding star, with his deep spirituality and his simple yet powerful and pure style. Danger, however, lay in Hesse's acquiring a vague, pantheistic aestheticism, and Hermann's parents were justified in worrying anew.

After completing three years of formal apprenticeship, Hesse remained as a clerk for an additional year. Much of his free time was now spent in writing. A few of his poems were accepted by magazines, although many more were returned. At his own expense Hesse published in 1899 his *Romantic Songs* (*Romantische Lieder*), a poetic collection filled with melancholy and nostalgia.

Hesse's next work found a publisher in Eugen Diederichs, whose fiancée Helene Voigt, herself a fine writer, had pleaded with her future husband to accept the manuscript. It was the prose collection *An Hour Beyond Midnight* (*Eine Stunde nach Mitternacht*, 1899). The enigmatic title was meant to suggest a mood of aesthetic seclusion. In spite of traces of immaturity and a certain dependence on Maeterlinck, the book showed some promise, which was recognized by no less a critic than young Rainer Maria Rilke. It also served Hesse as a fitting introduction to the *petit cénacle*, a Tübingen association of student aesthetes, of whom Ludwig Finckh, the later writer of sweet poetic prose, would prove the most enduring comparison.

The *petit cénacle* group was typical of German youth before World War I. Many young people of finer sensibilities felt lost in the new German Empire which from 1888 was personified in the youthful, neurotic Emperor Wilhelm II. These sons and daughters of simple, hard-working middle-class families merely wished to continue the regional culture of their forefathers. They were uncomfortable in the Wilhelmine age of industrial expansion and world politics, of burgeoning cities, of civil discontent and rebellious socialists. To be sure, a few of the new writers like the alert Silesian Gerhart Hauptmann or the honest Bavarian Ludwig Thoma found themselves in active opposition and openly voiced their political sympathies. In the big cities there were many trenchant critics of the new regime and many readers of liberal and radical magazines and newspapers. But there were also many bewildered youths who were gradually withdrawing from the ugliness and class-consciousness of modern civilization and seeking islands of inner peace and Romantic forgetfulness.

The so-called Youth Movement started before 1900 with the founding of the Steglitz *Wandervögel* ("migratory birds") by Karl Fischer. In the first decade of the new century many youth groups could be met roaming over the countryside with their sooty cooking utensils and heavy rucksacks; with their beribbonned guitars and their repertoire of ancient folk songs. They imitated the wanderings of medieval students and of nineteenth-century journeymen, cultivated romantic friendships, and led a simple, unpretentious life. They read the regional writers who from 1900 on had drawn together in a *Heimatkunst* movement in defiance of so-called hothouse and asphalt literature. The *Heimatkunst* poets perpetuated the village and country tales of an earlier period—the literature of the Swiss masters Jeremias Gotthelf and Gottfried Keller, the Swabians Eduard Mörike and Berthold Auerbach, the Silesian Joseph von Eichendorff, the North Germans Fritz Reuter and Theodor Storm. Young Hesse seemed to belong among these regional writers, and his membership in the *petit cénacle* stamped him as a romantic escapist. Until 1914 there was little evidence in his writing to refute that image.

On August 31, 1899, Hesse's Tübingen years came to an end. He spent a happy holiday in the Swabian mountains, one which even left room for a mild romantic interlude. But then he set out for a new position in a bookstore at Basel, the provincial center of cultural and historical traditions which held a singular attraction for him. His baggage contained a framed reproduction of *The Isle of the Dead* by Arnold Böcklin, a native of Basel, and the works of Nietzsche, who had once taught there.

Böcklin stood for a romantic aestheticism which populated nature with mythological figures. His original paintings in the Basel Art Museum were to open Hesse's eyes to the lively colors of southern nature, and his *Vita Somnium Breve* (Life is but a short dream) was to become a guardian image. Nietzsche stood for vigorous, outspoken style, and for a thoroughly critical attitude toward bourgeois hypocrisy and traditional Christianity. The latter's influence was at first overwhelming, but in time it yielded to the more subtle attraction of Jakob Burckhardt. Although Burckhardt had died in 1897, his spirit was still a vital part of the Basel atmosphere. The sage author of *The Culture of The Renaissance* and of *Constantine the Great* engendered in Hesse an unsentimental concept of reality and was the only historian successful in winning the young writer's confidence and veneration. It was through Böcklin's and Burckhardt's eyes that Hesse viewed the neighboring Swiss Alps and, in 1901, experienced Italy.

The poet's altered concept of life found its first expression in *The Posthumous Papers and Poems of Hermann Lauscher* (*Hinterlassene Schriften und Gedichte von Hermann Lauscher*, 1901). This small book is pervaded by romantic *fin de siècle* melancholy, but already foreshadows a more positive attitude toward reality, with a stress on conscious progression toward clear vision. It also evidences the beginning of a simpler style, with deliberate use of the picturesque adjective.

In September 1901, in order to free himself for more literary work, Hesse exchanged his Basel position for a less demanding one in Calw. It was here that his literary fame began. In 1902 the well-known poet Carl Busse edited 200 of Hesse's poems, presenting them with a sympathetic introduction, and the writer Paul Ilg was so impressed by the prose of *Hermann Lauscher* that he recommended the young author to the Berlin avant-garde publisher Samuel Fischer. Hesse sent the publisher the story of *Peter Camenzind*, which in 1903 was printed in Fischer's magazine *Neue Rundschau* and in 1904 appeared as a separate book.

The novel met with enthusiastic acclaim and made its author famous overnight. The royalties from *Peter Camenzind*, which were augmented by honoraria for poems and other contributions to literary magazines, enabled Hesse to give up the book trade and establish himself as a free-lance writer. This step was also necessary for reasons of health. Hesse's vision was so poor that he could not tolerate prolonged eyestrain, which was unavoidable in the book trade. He was often subject to the same neuralgia from which his father had suffered. In 1900 the draft board gave the poet its lowest classification.

In 1902 Hesse's mother died. Two years later he married Maria Bernoulli, a Basel photographer nine years his senior, who came from a well-known family of mathematicians. The Hesses moved to Gaienhofen on Lake Constance.

The novel *Peter Camenzind*, which made this move possible, appeared at a time when the young generation of German writers was turning to Impressionism, a style created by French painters of the eighteen-sixties and -seventies. Influenced by an avowed sensualism, it emphasized atmospheric elements, and moved by the simplicity of Far Eastern art, it cultivated the pure line. Impressionism also was occupied with atmosphere and rhythmical irregularity. This opened new possibilities to the poetic individual and led to interesting personal styles. It represented an important modification of traditional nineteenth-century Realism, but was by no means a complete break with it. It could therefore blend readily with certain older, Romantic elements. Many such unions of Impressionism and neo-Romanticism were attempted by the Vienna group of writers (Arthur Schnitzler, Hugo von Hofmannsthal, Peter Altenberg, Richard Beer-Hofmann, and others), by the North German Thomas Mann, by the Silesian Carl Hauptmann, and by the Swabians Ludwig Finckh and Emil Strauss.

Hesse's *Peter Camenzind* fitted admirably into these literary developments. It concerned a young man who had become dissatisfied with civilization in general, and not simply with its modern form. In the novel, he stands at that point of his life where he is just discovering the hypocrisy of many adults and the emptiness of so many minds and careers. But the society against which the young man protests is essentially the German society of the eighteenth century that had continued almost without change to the end of the nineteenth. Many peasants and craftsmen appear in the story, but no modern industrial laborers are included. To be sure, Peter Camenzind sometimes uses the railroad for his journeys; but his travels would not have essentially changed if he had used the mail coach. Telephone conversations and telegrams remain unheard-of luxuries, lake steamers are bypassed in favor of rowboats. The automobile and the aeroplane of course do not yet exist. We hear a great deal about St. Francis and Novalis, of Gotthelf and Keller, but nothing of Marx or Darwin. Nietzsche and Wagner are mentioned only in passing.

Peter Camenzind's problem is an age-old one: How can a sensitive boy newly aware of the world's perfidy find his true place in society?

At the outset of the story he is a goatherd in Nimikon, a village on Lake Constance, and lives in eternal communion with the forces of nature. The monks of a nearby cloister discover that Peter is talented and prevail upon his father to send him to school on a scholarship. Peter becomes enamoured by the world of books and devotes most of his free time to day-dreaming and writing. As a gifted village boy he is later sent to Zurich University on another small scholarship, which he augments by writing for newspapers. Peter ekes out an existence by living frugally, but his greater problem is to overcome his sensitive isolation. He makes friends with an older and more worldly student, who is drowned just as the friendship reaches a point of true understanding.

He seeks the companionship of young women. But he does not have the courage to speak to his first dream girl. His second inamorata tells him of her impending engagement at the point when he is ready to confess his love. He withdraws for such a long time from the third girl that she meanwhile finds another life partner. And when a very practical and down-to-earth match is proposed to Peter by a motherly Italian widow, he in turn cannot accept the proposal. From then on he remains single and avoids contact with society as much as possible.

One cannot say that Peter does not try to find companions. When his friend Richard introduces him to a group of young Zurich intellectuals, Peter cannot bear their acid wit and their aesthetic arrogance. Later he submerges for a time in the Paris *bohème*, but his healthy peasant character soon becomes surfeited with its questionable joys. Again and again Peter seeks solace in lonely wanderings, which lead him to Lombardy, Tuscany, Umbria, and Southern France, each with its more natural and friendly people. Or he drinks for forgetfulness in taverns. After his Paris excesses Peter's isolation reaches such a degree that he has to seek medical help.

This untenable situation is alleviated only when Peter moves to Basel and builds friendships with people who are removed from the intellectual and artistic life. He associates with a simple cabinet-maker and his family. He shares their innocent joys and their profound sorrow over the death of their young daughter. And here he meets the hunchback Boppi, who is avoided by healthy people.

Peter Camenzind tries at first to get away from the pale and sickly cripple, until one Sunday his conscience is awakened. He then realizes that his avoidance of Boppi is incompatible with his loudly professed veneration for St. Francis. Peter makes an effort to draw Boppi into conversation. He takes him in a wheelchair to the zoo and finally rents a small apartment where they can live together. The hunchback discloses himself as a friendly and uncommonly wise person. He teaches Peter the value of resignation from the human and a sympathetic understanding of the animal world. When Boppi becomes seriously ill and has to be moved to a hospital, Peter not only pays his bills, but also visits him regularly and mourns his untimely death.

City life loses all attraction for the young journalist. He leaves Basel and returns to his home village to care for his father who has become a problem to his neighbors. Peter makes his father comfortable and repairs the house. When a village emergency arises from the devastations of a spring storm, Peter offers his services. He again finds a place for himself in village life and associates once more with his Uncle Konrad, who during Peter's childhood had amused him with many misguided "inventions." And all these new, and yet really old, obligations keep Peter busy enough without recourse to his literary work. He still spends some time on the manuscript of a novel, but it is doubtful if he will ever finish it.

It would be wrong to interpret the close of Peter Camenzind's autobiography as a withdrawal from life. It is, to be sure, a withdrawal from urban civilization and irresponsibility. But it is also a conscious acceptance of the small place in life which has been ordained to the individual. Peter, who in his beginnings was entirely preoccupied with the imagined importance of his avocation, who looked down on the villagers with subtle irony, and who shunned social contacts has, in the end, become an ordinary human being. He has not become a peasant boy again, nor yet a gentleman farmer, but he has learned to take the small duties of life seriously. He cooks his father's meals, he takes his old uncle to the village inn, he fixes his roof. Whatever he does, however, he lives on the fringe of society and is still something of an outsider.

This solution is not defeatism nor a renewal of Rousseau's withdrawal into nature. It also cannot be equated with *fin de siècle* nostalgia and regionalist rejection of the all-too-pressing and all-too-ugly realities of modern industrial civilization. It is rather a taking up of the humble life of St. Francis, for whom no domestic chore was too menial and no room and board too frugal in his quest for an imitation of Christ. Franciscan too is the love for nature and the empathy with animal life that helps to shape the book. There is a delightful conversation between a fox and a marten, which Boppi and Peter have invented to pass the time; there are admirable descriptions of the föhn blowing down from the Alps in the spring and awakening the restless impulses of the human body. There are wonderful cloud and lake descriptions:

> Show me in the wide world the man who knows the clouds better and loves them more than I! Or show me the thing in the world which is more beautiful than the clouds. . . . They hover like silver in a thin layer, they are sailing as a white laughter with a golden edge, they stand resting in yellow, red, and bluish colors. They are creeping darkly and slowly like murderers, they are chasing head over heels like mad, rushing riders, they hang sadly and dreaming in pale heights like melancholy hermits. They have the forms of enchanted isles and the shapes of blessing angels, they are like threatening hands, fluttering sails, wandering cranes. . . . They are the eternal symbol of all wandering, all searching, desiring, and longing for home. And as they are hanging timidly and longingly and defiantly between heaven and earth, thus the souls of men are hanging timidly and longingly and defiantly between time and eternity (I, 230).

This is the language of nature-mysticism, Hesse's answer to his religious problem up to the beginnings of World War I. One must avoid calling it pantheism, for pantheism means addressing nature or the cosmos or the universe as God. Hesse

shuns every personal image or definition of God, but he still
believes in the existence of a deity. Nature is its appearance,
but not its essence. The proper term for such a view, in which
God comes first and the universe second, is theopanism. Its
God, who defies human definition, is generally called the *deus
absconditus*. But this hidden God can be approached by mysticism, which can be either transcendent or immanent. If it is
transcendent, it approaches God by separation from the world
and by concentration upon whatever is experienced as his immediate presence.

Immanent mysticism, on the other hand, approaches God
by immersion in his appearance in nature, in his creatures, and
in the people he has created; in the personal activities he is
directing. This immanent mysticism was the mysticism of St.
Francis who addressed the wind and the clouds, the birds and
the fishes, the poor and the sick as his brothers. Hesse's own
mysticism in *Peter Camenzind* can also be called immanent, or
Franciscan.

Only by keeping such definitions in mind can one arrive at
an adequate understanding of Peter Camenzind's vacillation
between withdrawal into self and communion with nature;
between individual isolation and social concern. The immanent
mystic seeks God within nature and through the love of his
fellow-man. But he does not simply seek nature; he does not
simply seek company and love. If he did that, he would substitute them for God, an act which, of course, must be avoided.
So he hovers somewhere in between. Peter's absorption in the
clouds and in other atmospheric phenomena is typical. It allows
him to embrace nature without, however, embracing anything
too solid or too definite. Equally typical is his love for Elisabeth
whom he venerates deeply, but cannot approach personally:

Wie eine weisse Wolke	In the way a white cloud lingers
Am hohen Himmel steht,	In all the height of heaven,
So weiss und schön und ferne	So white, so fair, and distant,
Bist du, Elisabeth.	Elisabeth, thou art.
Die Wolke geht und wandert,	The cloud goes forth and
Kaum hast du ihrer acht,	wanders
Und doch durch deine Träume	(You hardly give it heed),
Geht sie in dunkler Nacht.	And yet throughout your
	dreaming
	It goes in darkling night.

Geht und erglänzt so silbern,	It goes and glows so silver
Dass fortan ohne Rast	That henceforth without rest
Du nach der weissen Wolke	For yon white cloud you harbor
Ein süsses Heimweh hast.	Sweet sighing in your breast.

$$(I, 339-340).$$

Immanent mysticism has also engendered the simplicity of Hesse's style. His images are clear and appropriate. They show wonderful observation and concentration, yet are never over-burdened with detail or oppressive with their earthiness. His sentences are simple and direct; they never confuse us with involved constructions and verbosities. An Italian landscape might be described as follows:

In happy exuberance we emptied the beakers of beauty and pleasure. We reached in our wanderings isolated villages on hot hills, we made friends with innkeepers, monks, girls, and small, satisfied village parsons, we listened to naive serenades, we fed pretty, brownish children with bread and fruit, and saw from sunny mountain heights Tuscany lying in the splendor of spring and the distantly glistening Ligurian Sea (I, 291).

The animals in the zoo are characterized by few but potent adjectives. The buffalo is called "gruff," the tapir, who takes his feed for granted, is labeled "the customs collector" (I, 348). Peter Camenzind describes his own appearance as a mature man with humorous detachment as the picture of a man with a strong nose and a surly mouth (I, 367). Old Uncle Konrad "continuously has his index finger in his mouth and a thinker's wrinkle on his forehead; he makes small hasty steps around his room and in clear weather looks often across the water" (I, 371–372).

All of these details are fitting and to the point, but they do not allow one to become immersed in reality. For the main concern of the novel is still the spiritual biography of its hero, exemplified by his changing states of mind, and therefore a certain lyrical quality predominates. It is to some extent merely a great confession, and Peter is Hermann Hesse's blood brother. Still the two must not be confused, and the story is properly called a "novel." It represents but one of Hesse's attempts to come to grips with the problem of reality.

One can understand why the story, with its stress on transient atmospheric phenomena and on the inner moods of

its hero, was interpreted as a manifestation of *fin de siècle*
Impressionism and was grouped with the writings of Eduard
von Keyserling and Cäsar Flaischlen, Ludwig Finckh and Emil
Strauss. It seemed to offer a literary parallel to the paintings of
Max Liebermann and Leopold von Kalckreuth.

The novel found its most enthusiastic readers among German youth. They felt that this was a writer of their own
generation who understood their sensitive recoil from modern
machine civilization and urban intellectualism; who like themselves was embracing a life of rusticity; a return to nature. The
story's effect was exhilarating and liberating, and Hesse was
loved for it during most of his life. In later years he had difficulty avoiding admirers who sought to type him as the author
of *Peter Camenzind.*

He tried in retrospect to spell out the differences between
his youthful hero's approach to life and that of the *Wandervögel.* He explained that the wandering students of the youth
movement sought release in friendship and attempted to build
up new communities, while Peter Camenzind became a pronounced individualist and withdrew into nature mysticism.
Hesse could have stressed the fact that his novel was no mere
repetition of Romantic and late Realist patterns taken over
from Keller and Eichendorff, but had benefitted immeasurably
from the devotion of modern impressionist art to pure lines
and vivid colors, to *plein-air* and atmospheric mood. But actually these differences were minor. There were many confirmed
individualists among the early *Wandervögel,* and they read
not only Keller and Storm but also Maurice Maeterlinck and
Nietzsche, Ruskin and Tolstoy. Hesse's identification with the
younger generation was more complete than he was willing to
admit.

3 · The Young Writer

Peter Camenzind reflected Hesse's early life in Basel and Swabia. His subsequent stories were to a large degree engendered by Gaienhofen and its surroundings; but many still took place in Gerbersau, which he used as a synonym for the town of Calw.

Hesse's first wife was sensitive and frail. She therefore supported Hesse's own desire to live in the country, away from modern civilization. So the young couple moved into a farm house in a secluded village in the quiet Gaienhofen region. Gas and electricity were unknown, and water had to be brought from a well. Yet even this modicum of comfort disturbed Hesse. He would jump up from his desk and roam the countryside for hours without aim or purpose.

Bruno, Hesse's first son, was born in the farmhouse in December 1905. Its quarters therefore proved too small, and Hesse gave into his wife's urging to build a house of their own. The new house was surrounded by a garden, which Hesse maintained. According to his back-to-the-soil principles, he sowed and harvested everything himself, planting trees and berry bushes, sunflowers and nasturtium vines.

The Hesses were not the only artistic couple who had found a home on Lake Constance. Close by lay the house of Dr. Ludwig Finckh, who in 1906 dedicated his idyllic *Rosendoktor* to Hermann Hesse. And in the course of the years many visitors found their way to Hesse's Rousseauan retreat. Their visits were not without painful consequences for some of them. Stefan Zweig received such a severe bump on his head from the low door on his first visit, that he had to lie down for fifteen minutes, before he was able to speak again. Painters like Max Bucherer, Hans Sturzenegger, and later Ernst Morgenthaler, sought Hesse's company. Hesse's wife, who was an accomplished pianist, attracted musical acquaintances. Othmar Schoeck, who set many of Hesse's songs to music, even solicited an opera text from the poet. The libretto, however, could not be used.

Thus the outside world did not permit Hesse to live in complete seclusion. He traveled to Zurich and even to Milan to listen to operas and symphonic concerts. The critics honored him with literary prizes and included his name in biographical dictionaries.

In Gaienhofen Hesse wrote the novels *Under the Wheel* and *Gertrude*, as well as the stories collected in *On Earth* (*Diesseits*, 1907), *Neighbors* (*Nachbarn*, 1908), and *Detours* (*Umwege*, 1912). He also became a contributor to many literary magazines and a regular book reviewer. He edited many older literary documents, among which the works of Jean Paul, of Hölderlin, and of Novalis were his favorites. Like the Austrian Hugo von Hofmannsthal, Hesse sought to foster a cultural revival by his editorial efforts. Of the poet's anthologies we may mention *The Linden Tree* (*Der Lindenbaum*), a collection of German folksongs gathered in collaboration with Emil Strauss and Martin Lang. Frequently the poet was invited to read from his poetry, public performances alien to his nature.

All of these activities do not appear to modify the image of young Hesse as a romantic regionalist. However, there was one exception. He signed from January 1907 until December 1912 as an editor of the semi-monthly (and later weekly) *März*, printed by the liberal Munich publisher Albert Langen. One other editor was Ludwig Thoma. *März* vigorously opposed the saber rattling and the cultural hypocrisy of the Wilhelmine minions. It was the serious brother of Langen's satirical weekly *Simplizissimus* that so delightfully ridiculed bureaucratic stupidity and bourgeois stuffiness.

Hesse contributed notes, stories, reviews, and long articles to both magazines. But he put his name on the masthead of the serious magazine, the title of which commemorated the liberal March Revolution of 1848 and also referred to the lusty March winds that its sponsors hoped would initiate a cultural springtime for Germany. By lending his name to *März*, Hesse identified himself with Thoma's and Langen's campaign for international peace and understanding.

When he gave up his editorial chair for greater concentration on his poetic work, Hesse continued his contributions for the new editor, Theodor Heuss, a South German liberal who after World War II became the first President of the new German Federal Republic. Hesse was not yet a political writer, but he already had pronounced liberal and pacifistic predilections and belonged to the opposition. The day was not far distant when his political ideas would find expression.

Hesse's resignation from the editoral staff of *März* was one indication that he was chafing under his immense burden of work. He also began to seek frequent release from the Gaienhofen existence by travel to Italy, the Swiss Alps, and Austria. In 1909 he visited the ailing Wilhelm Raabe in Brunswick, one of the few authors of German nineteenth-century literature whose writing seemed out of step with their time. In the same year Hesse's second son Heiner was born in Gaienhofen. His third son Martin was born in 1911, and this added to his responsibilities. He began to complain about depression and lack of understanding. Much of this inner condition was revealed in the poem *In the Fog* with the bitter ending:

Seltsam, im Nebel zu wandern!	Weird, in the fog to wander!
Leben ist Einsamsein.	Life means you're on your own.
Kein Mensch kennt den andern,	No man knows another,
Jeder ist allein.	Each one is alone.

(I, 636).

In 1911 the poet sought escape in a visit to India. It was the first indication of a crisis that came to a head with the outbreak of World War I in 1914. But let us pause here for a consideration of Hesse's narrative works after *Peter Camenzind*.

Hesse's freedom to become a writer and to live the unconventional life of a creative artist was gained only with difficulty, and one can therefore understand the concern of many of

his early stories with problems of adolescence and early love.
Again and again they treat a young man's struggle to assert
himself against a hostile world and to overcome timidity and
self-seeking infatuation in favor of mature, all-embracing identification with life and with the beloved.

The heroes of these stories are often young people of
Hesse's own class. Such, for example, is the awkward lover in
Harvest Moon (*Heumond*, 1905; I, 675–718) or the high-school
student in *The Latin Scholar* (*Der Lateinschüler*, 1906; I, 637–
674). The latter, reminiscent of Hesse's Göppingen days, falls
in love with a servant girl, who makes him realize the egotistical
character of his infatuation with her. In the end he has "no
better wish for himself than that he too at some future time
might love and be loved in the same holy way as the poor girl
and her fiancé" (I, 674).

In other stories Hesse introduces us to representatives of
the *petite bourgeoisie*, sons of craftsmen and store clerks such
as he himself had been in his book selling days. Thus we meet
Andreas Ohngelt in the humorous tale *The Engagement* (*Die
Verlobung*, 1908; II, 195–216). At thirty years of age, Ohngelt
still lacks self-confidence in the presence of women and has to
cover his embarrassment by evasive phrases and elaborate groom-
ing. When the girl of his daydreams ridicules him in an effort
to rid herself of an unwelcome lover, Ohngelt is tempted to
succumb to self-pity. But a manly act of confession wins him the
love of Pauline Kircher, a girl who had always adored him.

A more questionable character is Ladidel in the story of the
same name (1909; II, 260–312), a lazy, easygoing young man
who has not finished the *Gymnasium*, is bypassing the state
examination for notaries, and associates only with girls whom
he can approach without effort. He barely manages to stay on
the right side of the law and is on the way to becoming a drifter.
But a more practical friend puts him into the barber's trade,
and everything ends well for Ladidel.

He is more fortunate than *Emil Kolb*, the pleasure-loving
son of a cobbler (1911; II, 395–424). Kolb is not able to with-
stand temptation and finally steals for the sake of a girl who
is expecting his child. He is soon found out and put behind
bars, where he has time to reflect on his pointless drive for

recognition. An even weaker character is described in *Walter Kömpff* (1908; II, 217–259), who is unable to assert his independence at all and finally hangs himself.

In some of these stories the theme of *Peter Camenzind* is repeated wholly or in part. In the story *The Reformer* (*Der Weltverbesserer*, 1911; II, 430–467) one finds a clear parallel to Peter Camenzind's rejection of temperance unions in Bertold Reichardt's rejection of vegetarianism. In *The Homecoming* (*Die Heimkehr*, 1909; II, 313–354), the rejection of small-town gossip and astute philistinism is even more pronounced than in *Peter Camenzind*. In *Beautiful Youth* (*Schön ist die Jugend*, 1907; I, 719–761), Peter Camenzind's nostalgic return to his home town and his unsuccessful love affairs are repeated. Yet this time the frame of reference is more autobiographical.

The style of these stories is a typical *fin de siècle* mixture of Romanticism and Impressionism. One finds many lyrical elements of an outspokenly impressionistic character. Some are of little consequence, while others capture a mood successfully, like the fall meditation called forth by a reading of Mörike's poem *Septembermorgen* (*Herbstbeginn*, "Indian Summer," 1905). Comparable to the best chapters in *Peter Camenzind*, these stories are clothed in an atmospheric awareness typical of Impressionism and exhibit the Romantic fusion of music, beauty, and nature.

The best of these impressionistic pieces describes a hike in the fall (*Eine Fussreise im Herbst*, 1906; I, 604–636). Here the narrator wanders from a quiet village on the southern side of Lake Constance to Ilgenberg, in order to visit his former sweetheart Julia. But she is now married and has become a robust bourgeois matron. Full of contempt for her humdrum existence, the narrator continues on his journey and realizes his loneliness.

One must not, of course, simply equate the narrator of Hesse's first-person stories with the author himself. The problem of bridging the gulf between youth and society, or between irrational passion and sane planning for life, is too general and basic to all nature to be derived solely from an individual's personal experience. It reflects at once the beauty and the sadness of life, its sublimity and its brutality, and can be mastered only by an all-embracing artistic symbol. Such a symbol was found by Hesse in the powerful story *The Marble Saw* (*Die Marmorsäge*, 1904; I, 549–581). Here the marble mill by its very existence in the midst of a peaceful country valley affects us with a sense of strangeness and foreboding catastrophe. This time it is not a growing boy but an engaged girl who is disturbed by the discovery of a conflicting passion against which she is helpless. She tries to fight it, but in the end gives in and seeks death in the river.

Hesse found another fitting symbol of the disturbances of youth in the cyclones that occasionally harassed the South German landscape. In one of his stories (*Der Zyklon*, 1913; I, 762–780) a cyclone symbolizes the power of the elemental life urge which sweeps away a young man's sentimental attachment to his childhood and shapes him into an independent human being. It tosses him into the passionate embrace of a young town girl, who has for a long time secretly loved him and now fills him with trust and self-confidence. When the narrator of this vacation experience leaves his badly battered home town again, his mood is only mildly elegiacal, and he is ready to face life.

In order to gain artistic perspective, Hesse at other times tried his hand at fairy tales. In one of them a wandering youth meets his other self, which sings to him of the troubles awaiting him in the future and then vanishes. But the boy is not frightened and continues on his journey.

These artistic forms were not basically new. They had already been used by Gottfried Keller. The sober realism and regional humor of the Swiss master's *Seldwyla Stories* found their counterpart in many of Hesse's Gerbersau stories, although Keller's heroes as a rule were more earthy and less timid. The fairy-tale mood of Keller's *Seven Legends* was also taken up by the younger writer. And even the incisive social criticism of Hesse's second novel *Under the Wheel* (*Unterm Rad*, 1904) was by no means unusual with Gottfried Keller.

The title of Hesse's second novel is of course symbolic. Its hero does indeed fall out of the vehicle of education, which is supposed to carry him forward, and is overrun by its murderous wheels. The metaphor aptly indicates the mechanical character of this education and vaguely reminds the reader of the medieval method of execution by a wagon wheel on a rack.

The subject of the story is Hans Giebenrath's unsuccessful rebellion against the ruthless school system supported by Wilhelmine society. His father is a formidable representative of a materialistic and stupid bourgeoisie. He has no understanding for his gifted and sensitive son, although he provides for him and loves him after his own fashion.

Presumably in order to help Hans to a free education, but actually in order to satisfy their social ambitions, the teachers and clergy of the small town prepare him for the *Landexamen* by drilling him after class. Six days a week the delicate boy has to study until ten o'clock or midnight. Even his walks in the fresh air are supposed to be taken in the company of a book. Hans's nature rebels against this abusive treatment. He suffers from headaches and loss of appetite and has nightmares about his pedagogical tormentors. But he is too weak to assert himself and to manifest anything but impotent rage. Dutifully he attends the *Landexamen* and even passes with second highest honors.

Unfortunately, this does not give the hunted boy a respite. He is again plagued with so-called "voluntary" extra lessons in order to do honor to his home town. He offers no resistance and even gives up his favorite sports of fishing and swimming, in which he had excelled. Weakened by headaches Hans enters the rigid and demanding cloister school at Maulbronn. In the beginning he does well, but then he meets Hermann Heilner, a classmate who has managed to break the vicious circle and to become spiritually independent. Hermann, who is musically gifted, ridicules Hans as a grind. He himself cares very little about his studies, and Hans, as a token of his loyalty, also gives up his endeavors. When the school authorities become aware of this, they force the two friends to separate. Hermann thereupon runs away from the seminary, and Hans is so deeply affected by his renewed loneliness, that he collapses like an abused horse. No one at school shows the least understanding of his condition.

At home during his convalescence, Hans finds no sympathy either. He is abandoned by his father, by his rector, by his teachers. Not even his physician is aware of the emotional crisis the boy is passing through. Only the thought that he could end his hated existence at any desirable moment makes living somewhat tolerable. Even his first erotic experience proves disappointing.

Hans is sent to a machine shop as an apprentice, but as a former seminary pupil he cannot adjust to his new environment. Fellow artisans invite Hans to a party, where is overtaken by a mood of depression. He drinks more wine than usual and heads homeward in a daze. The next morning he is found dead in the river. Hans's death appears especially ironic in view of his fondness of the water and his prowess in swimming. The concluding scene finds the forces of the status quo as firmly entrenched as ever.

The story is only partly autobiographical and is mainly based on the unfortunate school experience of Hesse's younger brother Hans, who as a diffident introvert suffered agonies from the pedagogues who tried to instill in him efficient habits. Later in life Hans actually did commit suicide when he found that he could not adjust to industrial society. But all the biographical material is used only to express a vital personal problem. Hermann Heilner and Hans Giebenrath represent the author's two selves. Hermann Heilner in his outbursts of temper, in his indifference to formal studies, and also in his clear awareness of his personal goal, represents Hesse's creative moments. Significantly he shares the author's initials. Hans Giebenrath represents Hesse's doubts of himself, his moods of despondency, his early attempt to seek solace in nature. But Hans Giebenrath's fate shows that the author's existential problem cannot be solved by a romantic flight from reality. Giebenrath perishes because of his lack of will-power and self-assertion. To be sure, nature for a while regenerates him, but he cannot forever exist in isolation. As has been truly said, no man is an island unto himself. The faults of the society into which Hans Giebenrath was born are not to be minimized. But the responsibility for his death is not entirely on society.

The novel cannot be conveniently classified as another exercise in social accusation like Heinrich Mann's *Professor Unrat* (*The Blue Angel*, 1906), Emil Strauss's *Freund Hein* 1902), Friedrich Huch's *Mao* (1907), or Robert Musil's *Disturbances of the Pupil Törless* (*Verwirrungen des Zöglings*

Törless, 1906), which were all published at the same time. The motive of social accusation, to be sure, was very strong in Hesse's novel and was the main reason for the popularity of *Under the Wheel*, but its primary concern was with personal problems. The novel displays an elegiac mood rather than one of social accusation.

Still, *Under the Wheel* is more than the expression of a passive phase. In his attack upon institutionalized religion and orthodox righteousness, in his sympathetic though not uncritical portrait of Swabian Pietism, Hesse exhibits a healthy religiosity. It is also a sign of psychic health that nature is by no means conceived as a romantic dream. The delights and the excitements of fishing are rendered realistically. The description of the small town includes studies of the people on the other side of the railroad track as well as of Hans Giebenrath's somewhat coarse fellow artisans.

The style of the story is not naturalistic. Most of the people talk in standard German, not in Swabian dialect. It is characterized by an Impressionistic unity of mood. Although there are overtones of bitter sarcasm and benevolent irony, actual humor is employed sparingly. Only the unmistakable sympathy of the author with the hero and his friend Hermann varies the mood to any extent.

The disadvantage of this style is a certain lack of plasticity. In this respect even the characterization of Hans Giebenrath leaves much to be desired. Hesse concentrates on his people's minds and neglects their outward appearances. Still there is some attempt to achieve a more compelling picture. The set ways of the father are shown in a series of simple, direct sentences, and the typical schoolmaster is skilfully characterized by his employment of pedantic metaphor. On the whole, however, the style of *Under the Wheel* accents color and atmosphere rather than line and design, and one can already discover traces of the amateur painter into which Hesse later developed.

Similar criticism might be made concerning the style of the novel *Gertrude*, the other longer story Hesse wrote following *Peter Camenzind* (1909–1910). It is also related in theme to the other narratives of this period. For *Gertrude* is another story of a young man who finds himself. This time he is a

musician discovering the secret of artistic existence, and the
story is of general, exemplary import. Hesse has attempted to
create symbols detached from his own personal life, and the
novel can no longer be termed personal or provincial.

Yet this novel too is narrated in the first person. The hero,
Kuhn, begins by telling of his happy childhood, when he was
completely immersed in dreams of glorious musical fulfillment.
His first doubts of himself were aroused at the conservatory,
where the young violinist had to spend hours in tedious prac-
tising. Like most other students he sought release in wild,
boisterous amusements. At the end of one sleigh party a pretty
girl dared him to ride with her down a dangerously steep hill,
which had only momentary consequences for herself, but crip-
pled Kuhn for life.

He now discovers the solitariness of artistic existence, but
rebels against it for a long time. Kuhn is thrown back and
forth between radiant inspiration and bitter, black despair and
has to pay dearly for every new creation. His songs and sonatas
express the godless isolation of the modern individual, yet they
serve to introduce him to the gifted baritone Heinrich Muoth
who, leading an equally forlorn existence, is covering up his
loneliness with arrogance. After struggling for a time against
this demanding new friend, Kuhn is drawn more deeply into the
vortex of Heinrich's social and musical life. It is Muoth who
makes Kuhn's songs known to the public and arranges for the
first performances of his sonatas. It is Muoth who tears his
friend away from the drab life of a provincial violin teacher and
procures for him a position in a respectable orchestra in which
he achieves at least outward satisfaction.

Yet Kuhn's inner loneliness persists and is poignantly revealed when he becomes acquainted with Gertrude, the cultured daughter of a wealthy patron of the arts. She appears to
incorporate that harmony for which Kuhn has been striving in
vain, and her quiet loveliness attracts and soothes him. When
he receives an opera text, Gertrude helps him set it to music.
They become close friends, and one day Kuhn kisses her. But
he lacks self-confidence and never pursues his advantage. He
manages to write to her about his passion, but does not find the
courage to speak of it. He even destroys all his possible chances,

by introducing Gertrude to Heinrich Muoth when they need a male voice for the developing opera. The two fall in love, and Gertrude becomes Muoth's bride in a church ceremony for which Kuhn has written the music.

Kuhn is on the point of committing suicide when he is called home to the bed of his dying father. Thereafter he makes a valiant attempt to forget his personal sorrows by taking care of his widowed mother. Meanwhile his opera becomes a success.

Yet Kuhn's life remains one of unhappy isolation. Even his sacrifice of Gertrude proves to have been in vain. Gertrude cannot adjust to Muoth's sarcastic temperament, nor can she restrain him. In the end Heinrich takes his own life. But this does not change Gertrude's relationship with Kuhn. She continues in suffering aloofness, and Kuhn lives in solitary devotion to his art. Life is cruel and fickle, but men can rise above it by creating imperishable works of art and by unselfish understanding of the sufferings of others. Kuhn's ultimate trust is in God, albeit in a wholly inscrutable God.

On the whole, *Gertrude* is a weak repetition of *Peter Camenzind*. In spite of conscious efforts to the contrary, it is far less plastic and far less conclusive. The central idea that art is born of suffering and sets the artist apart from common society and ordinary happiness, finds early expression and is later only slightly deepened and modified. It also does not become quite clear whether art, in the tradition of aesthetic idealism, is a satisfactory substitute for life or whether the last solution to the problem of existence is a religious one. In comparison with *Steppenwolf*, where artistic existence is described as a curse—although an inescapable and bravely accepted one— *Gertrude* might even be described as Hesse's passing flirtation with Humanism.

He was not too deeply involved with *Gertrude* and therefore did not develop the characters in depth. Apart from his hero Kuhn, the other characters find sketchy attention at least. A few of them, like Muoth, are adroitly outlined, yet Gertrude, who has given the novel its name, is but a shadow of herself and remains a somewhat anemic symbol for the serene harmony of art attainable in inspired moments. Equally nebulous are the locales. It is significant that in eighteenth-century literary fashion, cities are designated by initials or described in such general terms as "the capital." One need only remember Hesse's colorful descriptions of South German life in some of the Gerbersau stories to realize what might have been. And his characterizations in *The Engagement, Ladidel,* and *Under the Wheel* are also superior to those in *Gertrude.* Perhaps he should have abbreviated the novel into a novella or a symbolic tale. He was no novelist in the ordinary sense, and although *Gertrude* cannot be termed autobiographical, his interest was almost exclusively concentrated on the central figure of his artistic brother Kuhn.

In Hesse's poems of this period an equally melancholic mood prevails. The romantic folksong-like quatrain with its alternate rhymes is still his preferred form of expression. Nature is still the mirror for the poet's mood. Late summer and autumnal pieces are the rule. Nostalgic loneliness is an ever-recurrent theme. The colors are faint and shadowy; the rhythm hesitant. There are, to be sure, exceptions. On a trip through the St. Gotthard tunnel Hesse can anticipate the pleasure of Italian parties (V, 451); he can forget himself in the "pure present" of a piazzetta (V, 475); he can be overwhelmed by the quiet serenity of Cremona architecture (V, 600). After all, young Hesse wrote monographs not only on *Francis of Assisi* (1904), but also on *Boccaccio* (1904). Some of his Italian pieces also recall the sculptured defiance of Conrad Ferdinand Meyer's poetry, and some break away from folksong tradition toward realistic description and conversational length. The same can be said about the poems written on the Indian journey (V, 558–566). But from such interruptions Hesse always returned to his lonely preoccupation with self. He was, though, trying to overcome it, and the trip to India as well as his next stories, *Rosshalde* and *Knulp,* gave evidence of this attempt.

4 · Chafing Under the Yoke

IN HIS LAST Gaienhofen years Hermann Hesse was an unusually busy and industrious writer. But he did not exactly relish some of his activities and repeatedly sought release in trips to Italy and Switzerland, to Austria and to Alsace. Now in 1911 he went on a longer journey to India. Such journeys before World War I were not uncommon among German writers and intellectuals who were seeking a better perspective through distance. The same desire was uppermost also in Hesse's mind, but for him India offered additional attractions. It was the land where his mother had been born and his father and grandfather had been active missionaries; it was the land from which so many unusual visitors and rare foreign curios had come to the family residence in Calw.

In September 1911 Hesse left Genoa by steamer. He was accompanied by the painter Hans Sturzenegger. The ship took the direct route through the Suez Canal to Ceylon and Singapore. There Hesse and his friend transferred to a small Dutch coastal steamer and proceeded to South Sumatra. A Chinese side-wheeler then took them up the Hari River and also to Palembang. Originally a longer sojourn on the Malay Peninsula and a side trip to the Malabar coast had been planned, but Hesse's health began to trouble him, and he realized that his linguistic preparation was far from satisfactory. So the journey was considerably shortened and did not leave many lasting impressions.

In his travel book *From India* (*Aus Indien*, 1913) Hesse

37

kept to the surface of things. Ceylon with its many colors
and odors reminded him of the *Thousand ond One Nights*.
Penang impressed him by the teeming life of its Hindu, Chinese,
and Malay quarters; by its stores filled with exotic curios and
its nights perfumed by a thousand candles. Mount Pedrotala-
galla on Ceylon evoked awed admiration of its views of palm
trees and birds of paradise, of rice plantations and strange
temple structures, of fertile river valleys and primeval forests.
Occasionally the many new impressions filled Hesse's sleep with
exciting dreams.

Yet as a quest for deeper inspiration, the journey was a
failure. To be sure, Hesse carried away a favorable impression of
the Chinese, whom he described as strong and confident of their
future. But the Hindus and Malayans were less appealing to
him. The contrast between the pure essence of Buddhism and
its actual practice proved too great. Everywhere there was misery and dirt. The villages smelled. The temple services were
commercialized and presented a caricature of worship. Hesse
found much to criticize in Indian religious practice and in the
Indian character. He later summarized his impressions as follows:

There remains the experience of a dream visit with distant ancestors,
a return home to the fairy-tale-like childhood of mankind, and a
deep veneration of the spirit of the East, which in Indian or Chinese
dress since then again and again came close to me and has become
my consolation and prophecy. For we aged sons of the West can
never return to the aboriginal humanity and paradisiacal innocence
of the primitive people; but a good return and fruitful renovation
beckons to us from that 'spirit of the East' which leads from Lao-tse
to Jesus (III, 851–852). . . . My way to India and China did
not need ships and railroads, I had to find all the magical bridges
myself. I also had to forego seeking there salvation from Europe.
I had to stop filling my heart with hostility to Europe and must
inscribe into my own heart and spirit the true Europe as well as
the true East. That has taken years after years, years of suffering,
years of unrest, years of war, years of despair (III, 857).

Still, the trip to India led to at least one important decision—to terminate the Rousseauan experiment of Gaienhofen
which had now become a false façade. Hesse thought of moving
to the Dresden suburb of Hellerau, which had become an

artists' colony, or to Munich, to Zurich, or Bern. Finally, in September 1912, he rented the house of the painter Albert Welti outside of Bern. The fanciful pictures of Welti, who had just died, had found a sympathetic admirer in Hesse. The poet's house had even furnished the subject of one of Welti's paintings, *The House of My Dreams*, which now hangs in the Basel Art Museum. Hesse later began a novel with a similar title. He somehow hoped to achieve in Bern a more harmonious existence without the pretense of rusticity, but still not too close to the noisy mainstream of modern life. For Hesse, Bern belonged to the same Alemannic territory in which he had always felt at home.

Yet his hope for a greater integration of his existence found little fulfillment. The year 1913 saw the appearance of his novel *Rosshalde* in the German family magazine *Velhagen und Klasings Monatsheft*; the book form followed a year later. Here Hesse for the first time spoke of his marital difficulties. His frequent trips abroad had, in part, been means to avoid facing up to the growing estrangement between himself and his family.

It would be wrong however to interpret *Rosshalde* principally as an autobiographical tale of marital incompatibility. The marital problem presents only the outward aspect of the more general question of an artist's relation to ordinary life, which is, in turn, basically the old religious problem: how to be in the world but not of it.

Peter Camenzind had solved this problem by assuming the aspect of a world priest. The musician Kuhn in *Gertrude* had likewise found a place on the sidelines of life which allowed him to avoid direct involvement. The painter Johann Veraguth in *Rosshalde* tried to combine the lives of an uncommitted artist and a responsible family man but found it impossible.

In the beginning of the novel we see him working in his own studio, while his wife Adele lives apart in the comfortable manor house of Rosshalde. They share only their meals. Veraguth has thought of a divorce in order to put an end to the daily frictions between his volatile artistic temperament and the entirely correct and humorless world of his wife. But their common love for seven-year-old Pierre has so far held the couple together.

The arrival of Veraguth's boyhood friend Otto Burkhardt brings things to a head. Burkhardt has come from East Asia, which in his tales appears as a rich, colorful paradise. He entices Veraguth to accompany him there.

It was not only the splendor of tropical seas and island coasts, the abundance of forests and rivers, the colorfulness of half-naked children of nature, which created a longing in him and enchanted him by their images. It was even more the distance and calmness of a world in which his sufferings, his worries, his battles and deprivations must become strange and distant and pale, where a hundred small daily burdens would fall from his soul and a new, still pure, innocent, and unsuffering atmosphere would encompass him (II, 504).

To persuade Johann to follow his longings, Burkhardt shows him wonderful photographs of India and advises him to give up Pierre, for whom his mother will fight anyway and who will need his father far less than Veraguth has imagined. Veraguth promises to take the matter under consideration. After Otto's departure he paints, as a symbol of his problem, a portrait of a couple separated by a child at play. He becomes increasingly lonely and feels more and more superfluous. Even Pierre no longer needs him.

Then Pierre's elder brother comes home on vacation and takes him for a ride. The little boy returns in a state of morbid sensitivity and soon shows unmistakable symptoms of cerebral meningitis. In spite of a few sane moments the boy's condition worsens daily and he finally dies in dreadful convulsions. Before his death Adele once more tries to reconcile with her husband, but the attempt results in failure, and they separate.

In the procreation of this boy after years of bitter marital strife, Veraguth for the first and only time in his life forgot self and experienced true love. Now his love has died with its symbol and has left him in a void. "Much later and perhaps in a more bitter mood than other men do, he had taken leave from the sweet twilight of youth. Now he stood in the bright daylight as a poor latecomer, and he no longer wanted to lose one precious hour of it" (II, 633).

So the novel ends in frustration, leaving only a vague hope for the future. The call of India still remains. Veraguth's intention to take life more seriously and to give up his isolation is apparent. But one can scarcely know what will follow. The novel leaves the reader with little satisfaction and, possibly for this reason, had only a moderate success. Thus its importance is mainly personal to Hesse's development. It represents a step away from the sheltered nature mysticism of his early years and a step forward into the pitiless soul-searching of his middle period. For once he has dared to be as conclusive as he could. One might even interpret his novel as a vicarious anticipation of his own divorce, which came many years later.

It also represented a step forward in his artistic development. Hesse later maintained that with this book he reached a point of craftsmanship beyond which further advance was impossible for a man of his talents. With *Rosshalde* he succeeded in the perfect integration of story and symbol, of symbol and meaning. Hesse can now manage his plot with a few characters. He no longer needs the many figures of *Peter Camenzind* or even the substantial number of persons in *Gertrude*. The descriptive passages likewise are closely interwoven with the rest of the fabric, and are fraught with meaning. The adjectives are always potent; the sentences always clear.

Had the writer arrived at a dead end? An inspection of his next book *Knulp* would tend to confirm this suspicion. To be sure, it appeared in 1915, after the outberak of the great war which for Hesse signified a turning point in his life. But its roots reach back into the prewar period. Actually, one of its parts was first printed in 1908.

A superficial reading might easily mistake *Knulp* for a simple reshaping of the wanderer motif that has been part and parcel of the German Romantic heritage since Ludwig Tieck's *Wanderings of Sternbald* and Eichendorff's *Life of a Good-for-Nothing*. But there is one significant difference. The heroes of the traditional stories are wandering journeymen or medieval goliards, or even simple travelers, while Hesse's Knulp is a modern tramp. The romantic idyl had become somewhat stale, althought it was still portrayed by second-rate authors like Waldemar Bonsels (*Menschenwege*, 1918) or Horst Wolfram Geissler (*Der liebe Augustin*, 1921), who were almost certainly inspired by Hesse's example. But compared with the Knulp type, their heroes emerge as sugary philosophers or amiable relics of the past.

The real vagabonds of the machine age had already been portrayed in Hesse's story *In the Old Sun* (*In der alten Sonne*) contained in *Diesseits* (1905; I, 781–892). The title *In the Old Sun* was taken from the name of a dilapidated inn that the townspeople had transformed into a poorhouse. Its first inmates were a bankrupt locksmith and a former rope maker, who were both ruined by drinking. Then a demented poor devil by the name of Holdria and a crafty professional hobo named Tintenbein (Inky Leg) appear on the scene. Eventually the alcoholic locksmith hangs himself, and Tintenbein manages to escape with forged papers. For a while Holdria stays alone, until other derelicts arrive. Theirs is a world without promise, they are merely modern life's flotsam and jetsam.

Compared with Holdria and Tintenbein, Knulp, Hesse's later hero, is a good-looking man of high moral principles and clean habits. A sensitive introvert like Peter Camenzind and Hans Giebenrath, he also is unable to cope with the complexities of civilization and becomes a knight-errant of the road, pursuing mid-nineteenth-century traditions in modern surroundings. A heartless jade destroys his faith in mankind. To be sure, he finds other girls and even becomes the father of an illegitimate son, but he can never get over his first experience and never settles down to a steady occupation. In his self-pity Knulp feels superior to people and does not want to be beholden to them. Still he is a gifted whistler, an accordian player, and a verse-maker, whose company is frequently sought.

This style of life appeared tolerable during Knulp's youth, but becomes a problem in his later years. When we first meet him he has already contracted consumption and has run away from the hospital where he had gone to be cured. He is forced to live on the generosity of his friends, but tries not to take advantage of them and to contribute his share to their daily housework. He also avoids entanglements with their wives and cheers up homesick servant girls.

When Knulp feels his end approaching, he is seized with a powerful urge to visit once more the Swabian land of his youth. He walks the streets of his childhood and loses himself in reminiscences. He thinks that his whole life would have been different, if Franziska had not jilted him. "At that time he had thrown himself away and had not wanted to hear any more of love, and life had agreed and had not demanded anything. He had become an outsider, a loafer and onlooker, popular in his good young years, and lonely in the sickness of his old age" (III, 88).

Winter sets in, but still Knulp cannot resign himself to going to the hospital. He stays in the fields and the forests and resigns himself to approaching death. In his last hours God comes to him in a dream and reminds him of the fine days he had spent in his youth. He had many a girl friend and enjoyed many a Sunday dance.

Don't you see that you have had to be a light-minded person and a vagabond, so you could carry everywhere a little bit of childhood foolishness and of childhood laughter? . . . I have not been able to use you differently than you were. In My name you have wandered and have had to bring to the sedentary people a little bit of nostalgia for freedom. In My name you have committed foolishness and have allowed people to ridicule you; I Myself was ridiculed in you and loved in you. You were My child and My brother and a piece of Me, and you have neither enjoyed nor suffered anything that I have not also enjoyed and suffered in you (III, 95–96).

And Knulp resigns himself to dying in the snow. In his last moments the voice of God sounds to him like the voice of his mother or of the girls he has loved.

There was not enough material in Knulp's life for a novel, so Hesse confined himself to treating it in three short stories. Each one sketches an episode of Knulp's life, and by their arrangement Hesse managed to add some variety and suspense to an otherwise drab and undistinguished existence. Knulp is not depicted as a saccharine ideal, and his faults are not minimized. Still, the author has succeeded in arousing our sympathy and in somehow presenting Knulp as a minor brother of St. Francis. But he is not simply a link to Hesse's first novel *Peter Camenzind*. In his more mature work he anticipates Goldmund, the irresponsible wanderer and lover who has become a symbol for the creative life as against the equally essential contemplative life.

With the medieval scenes of *Berthold* (1908; I, 831-885) Hesse had already made another effort in this direction. Both early stories display the basic restlessness of Hesse in the last years before World War I and, together with *Rosshalde*, indicate that his artistic existence had become a problem to him.

On the other hand, Hesse retained from his early period his keen ability for close nature observation and the delicate simplicity of style first formed by Wilhelm Wackenroder and Novalis. His achievement presents Impressionism at its best, where the line dominates and the merely picturesque recedes behind bold strokes of the drawing pen. Hesse's public loved him for crystal-clear lines like the following:

There was a soft breeze in the air, and at times stars appeared in the black sky. . . . Near the gymnasium Knulp stopped and looked around. The moist wind whistled weakly in the leafless chestnut trees, the river flowed silently in deep blackness and reflected a few lit-up windows. The mild night benefitted the vagabond in all his fibers, he breathed feelingly and scented spring, warmth, dry roads and wandering. His inexhaustible memory was over surveying the town, the river valley, and the whole region, he knew his way around everywhere, he knew streets and footpaths, villages, hamlets, farms, familiar night lodgings (III, 38).

Or take the description of fall at the beginning of the third story where an October landscape is sketched in a few apt sentences:

It was a bright day in October. . . . On the highway to Bulach rode slowly the one-horse carriage of Doctor Machold. The way went gradually upwards. At the left were mown acres and potato patches, where the harvesting was still going on. At the right was a young, dense fir forest. . . . The road was leading directly forward into the bluish fall sky, as if the world had its upper end in it (III, 66).

Occasionally we also have lyrical verse in the customary manner of the Romantic novella. These poems serve to express what cannot be put down more rationally and help to enhance a mood. No wonder, then, that Hesse's *Knulp* was hailed everywhere as a legitimate revival of the Romantic tradition and found favor with the followers of the German youth movement who affected a similar style of life!

Yet for Hesse himself, Knulp's vagabondage was later destined to assume a more personal as well as a more artistically symbolic meaning.

5 · The End of an Era

THE OUTBREAK of World War I in August 1914 impressed the European reality on Hesse's mind and made permanent a feeling he had carried away from India: that escape from the modern age was impossible.

Seen from today's perspective the mobilizations of August 1914 concluded an era of western culture and initiated a turbulent new chapter, in which Christian Humanism was temporarily extinguished and Communism, Facism, Nazism, and state Socialism were presented as possible substitutes. But in 1914 most of these movements were very much in the future, and to the people of that day, the outbreak of war appeared in a wholly traditional light.

Everywhere in Europe the war was hailed as a liberation from meaningless routine and a return to the heroic values of the past. Every nation of Europe felt itself attacked and rallied to the defense of its national shrines. In Germany the war became a holy crusade in defense of the fatherland. Divisions between social classes and political parties disappeared overnight. Young men did not wait to be drafted but volunteered for military service in uncountable numbers. Similar results also occurred in Austria, in France, and in England. To be sure, in every country of Europe there were lonely seers like the German Georg Heym, who even before the war had harbored visions of a fiery god of destruction.

There arose some active opponents of the great conflagration, like the Frenchman Jean Jaurès who, because of his pacifism, was assassinated by superpatriots. Another pacifist was Jaurès' fellow countryman Romain Rolland, who for years had worked for a reconciliation between France and Germany. But these were exceptions without the power to stem the tide of irrational mass hysteria.

Hesse was also swept along by the maelstrom at first. He offered his services in the military reserve but was rejected for physical reasons. Later he was assigned to the German embassy in Bern for service in caring for German prisoners of war.

Yet when the tidal wave of German war poetry was thundering against the Swiss bastions, Hesse realized where he belonged spiritually and raised his voice against the spirit of war. Struck to the quick he published an article in the *Neue Zürcher Zeitung* of November 3, 1914, under the revealing title *Oh Freunde, nicht diese Töne!* (Oh friends, no sounds like these! VII, 44–49.) The article deplored the defection of most German intellectuals to the camp of the superpatriots and pleaded in passionate sobriety for an upholding of the historic standards of German culture. It sought dedication with renewed vigor, not to the defeat of foreign nations but to the defeat of unreasoning war and of modernized brutality.

The article, which to a later generation might appear moderate or even conciliatory, provoked Hesse's German contemporaries to fury. He was pilloried as a defeatist and insulted as an unpatriotic pacifist, a deserter from the common cause, a traitor, and partisan of the enemy. Overnight the poet lost friends and acquaintances. He saw his books disappear from the windows of the booksellers and suffered from the deliberate defection of his former readers. Only a few German friends, like the *März* editors Theodor Heuss and Conrad Haussmann, attempted to shield Hesse against the war hysteria, and he received an appreciative letter from the great French pacificist Romain Rolland. He warmly welcomed this comrade in arms and later dedicated the collection of his war essays to Rolland. Hesse kept aloof from other war opponents like the emigrants René Schickele and Leonhard Frank or the Zurich Dadaists. He decried radical pacifism as a negative attitude and did not believe that any organization could help modern man out of his predicament.

Without Rolland's moral support, Hesse's isolated opposition to the war might have ended in a mental breakdown. Now, however, he preserved his courage and pleaded again and again for an early end to the hostilities and a return to peace; for an avowed rededication to the eternal values of culture. War, he said, could never solve any problems. It led only to abnormal, schizophrenic conditions. The longer the war lasted, the more urgent became Hesse's pleas. In December 1917 he called its continuation nonsense. In 1918 he depicted the colored people and the oriental nations as ridiculing their enlightened European brothers (*Der Europäer* [The European], 1918; VII, 104–112).

Meanwhile, Hesse had become involved in the effort to alleviate the lot of the German prisoners of war. Together with the German ambassador in Bern, Prof. Richard Woltereck, Hesse became an official director of the book center for German prisoners of war from 1915 to the end of 1919. The center was financed in part by the German government, but also depended on voluntary contributions. Hesse wrote numerous letters to friends and colleagues, to librarians and publishers, asking for their support. The books they sent were classified and forwarded to the various French camps for prisoners of war. Later a series of 22 inexpensive reprints was brought out under Hesse's editorship. He also contributed the lion's share of work to the *Sonntagsbote für deutsche Kriegsgefangene* (Sunday Messenger for German Prisoners of War), published by the neutral Bern foundation *Pro captivis*. Together with Professor Woltereck he bore the responsibility for the *Deutsche Interniertenzeitung* (Newspaper for German Internees) distributed by the German Office for Prisoners of War.

The labor in time became a real burden and was aggravated not only by the mental disturbances caused by the war, but also by additional personal crises. First Hesse's youngest son became seriously ill. Then in 1916 his father died, and Hesse had to travel to Germany in order to attend the funeral and to assist in the execution of his father's will. Finally his married life became an ever greater strain. His wife Maria suffered a mental breakdown and had to be confined to an institution. In the first months of 1916 Hesse's own physical and psychic depression reached the danger point and forced him to interrupt his work in Bern. Writing became unbearable to him, and he could not even tolerate music.

The poet first sought relief in Locarno and Brunnen, and then turned in desperation to the Lucerne private clinic of Sonnmatt. Here he met Dr. Josef Bernhard Lang, a disciple of the psychologist Carl Gustav Jung. Lang soon became Hesse's intimate friend and treated him in some sixty sessions. These were not formal psychoanalytic consultations but rather intimate conversations between a disturbed poet and a sympathetic friend. In addition, Lang introduced his patient to the writings of Freud and the latter's erstwhile pupil Wilhelm Stekel, thus opening up an entire new world to him.

It must be remembered that in 1916 psychoanalysis was still a very controversial discipline. But Hesse was singularly well prepared for its revolutionary findings by his intimate acquaintance with the German Romanticists, who had been the first to realize the importance of dreams and to try to integrate them into a total picture of human life. He did not find it too difficult to understand dreams, in the psychoanalytic manner, as paths to the subconscious, which held the clue to most of man's riddles.

Psychoanalysis confirmed Hesse in his new feeling that evil and ugliness could not be avoided and lay deep in man's own soul. According to Freud, sexual urges played a dominant part from man's childhood, and all neuroses and psychoses could be reduced to sexual maladjustments. According to Jung, the human soul was built up of various layers of consciousness. Below the conscious male *animus* lay the suppressed heterosexual component, the "shadow" of the weaker *anima*, usually imagined in an ugly, cruel, sickly, or feeble form, as a whore, a female lackey, a she-wolf, or a lioness.

On a deeper level, this negative image of the *anima* was compensated for by the positive image of the inspiring guide or motherly friend, the selfless teacher or uplifting angel, in the form of Dante's "Beatrice" or of Hermes Psychopompos. Beneath this level of subconsciousness was an even greater image, the most comprehensive and ultimately satisfying of all: the union of the formerly hostile principles, the hermaphrodite god, the holy family of the God-father and the Madonna, the triune mystery of God the Father, God the Son, and God the Holy Ghost, usually visualized in the form of a mandala. The psychoanalyst of the Jungian persuasion aimed at leading his patient through the various layers of the subconscious to the visualization of this mandala, where his superficial conscious personality had its roots and could therefore reorient and reintegrate itself.

In his description of the human soul, Jung used many examples from poetry and religious imagery. He propounded the theory that the deepest levels of the soul were historically the oldest. Its myths preserved primal experiences and states of the human race, and were archetypes worthy of genuine veneration. For a long time Hesse attempted to follow Jung's path to integration, until he realized that introspection alone would never lead to salvation. It was then that Hesse widened Jung's individualistic approach to sanity into the social approach culminating in *The Bead Game*.

Psychoanalytic concepts helped Hesse considerably. They also serve as a key to a better understanding of his later works. But he did not become an amateur psychologist who used psychoanalysis namely for artistic purposes.[1] It made him more aware of the role of the subconscious in artistic creation. Life and thought now appeared as a battle between conscious and

1 We have recently witnessed a flurry of attempts to interpret literature in half-understood Freudian terms. Contemporary psychological research has also brought new explanations of Freud's monumental discoveries which differ from those of their originator. C. G. Jung has measurably added to these discoveries, but has not arrived at completely satisfactory theories either. The author is no competent judge of these theories and has therefore avoided a minute psychoanalytical interpretation of Hesse's works and development. He has preferred a philosophical and religious approach, which seems entirely defensible in view of the fact that Hesse's own motivation was primarily metaphysical. The author's approach would also agree with the recent "anthropological" interpretation of psychoanalysis, if it should meet with the specialists' acceptance (cf. Arië Sborowitz and Ernst Michel, eds. *Der leidende Mensch. Personale Psychotherapie in anthropologischer Sicht*. Düsseldorf-Köln: Diederichs, 1960). Strictly traditional Freudian psychoanalysis would contribute little to an understanding of Hesse's works as literature. If, however, psychologists want to use literary works and writers' biographies for their own purposes, they are entirely welcome, so long as they know their limitations and do not indulge in literary criticism.

subconscious tendencies, and a total picture of man emerged
which no longer was simple or one-sidedly rational.

I found all the war and the murderous greed of the world, all
its lightheadedness, all its raw thirst for pleasure, all its cowardice
within myself. I first had to lose my self-esteem, then my self-hate.
I had to do nothing else but endure the view into the chaos to the
end, in the often glowing, and often fading hope to find beyond
the chaos again nature and innocence. Every wideawake and conscientious man goes this narrow way through the desert once or
several times, it would be a vain effort to try to discuss it with
others (IV, 480).

There is no longer any desire to escape, be it into nature,
as Peter Camenzind and Knulp tried to do, or into art, as Kuhn
and Veraguth had attempted. The outbreak of the war had
proved to Hesse that he was no mere outsider and that its was
impossible for him to set himself apart. He must face himself
without evasions if he wanted to solve the problem of contemporary civilization. His new intention was to accept instead
of to suppress or forget. It was this intention that signified a
complete break with Hesse's past.

The sessions with Dr. Lang helped Hesse to bring to the
surface all the dreams and frustrations that were lodged in his
subconscious. He took the royal road to the "Mothers," as
Goethe in his Faust called the matrices of artistic creation.
Dream sequences were incorporated in many of the Fairy Tales
(Märchen) of 1919, one of which is actually called Eine
Traumfolge (A Dream Sequence, 1916; III, 328–341) and
relates an unsuccessful attempt to find integration with the
subconscious mother image. Another, entitled Faldum (1915–
1916; III, 342–363), symbolizes the frustration resulting from
the wish to set oneself apart from human misery. An earlier
one, The Poet (Der Dichter, 1914; III, 286–293), goes back
to 1914 and speaks of the impossibility of capturing life's fulness
in self-contained images. The poet of this tale cannot yet achieve
complete integration.

Yet the subconscious also comprises unfulfilled hopes and
prototypes of things to come. The story entitled Strange News
from a Distant Star (Merkwürdige Nachricht von einem andern
Stern, 1915; III, 302–320) evokes the irrepressible hope for

eternal peace in spite of all setbacks. And in the wonderful fairy
tale *Augustus* (1913; III, 261–285) the hero regains the angelic
peace of his childhood by giving up his desperate struggle for
recognition and forgetting self in the service of others. In the
end, like the hero of Franz Kafka's *Castle*, he falls asleep in the
arms of an old man, i.e., he identifies himself with his psychopompos. In the story *The Steep Road* (*Der schwere Weg*, 1917;
III, 321–327), destiny is faced in another form, that of a
motherly divinity with whom the narrator finally unites.

Perhaps Hesse's most satisfactory use of psychoanalytic
imagery is found in *Iris* (1918; III, 364–383), the story most
likely to have been written at the successful end of Hesse's
psychoanalytic treatment. The imagery is strongly reminiscent
of an episode in Novalis' *Disciples of Sais*, namely, the famous
fairy tale of "Hyacinth and Little Rosebud." In other words,
Hesse has found it possible to face his Romantic past and to
reinterpret it in the light of his newly acquired insight.

In the story of *Iris* Anselm, looking for the meaning of life,
falls in love with Iris, his "Beatrice." She, however, does not
want to marry him, since his soul does not harmonize with hers.
While Anselm continues his quest, Iris falls ill and dies, leaving
him the flower bearing her name as a symbol. In the end Anselm
comes to the gate of the spirit world. Walking through it, he
forgets himself and thus reaches his goal. The disappearance
of Iris here signifies the narrator's identification with his "Beatrice" and the overcoming of his schizoid existence. It parallels
the meaning Novalis intended to convey when he told how
Hyacinth and Little Rosebud finally sank into each other's
arms.

These fairy tales no longer allow a realistic or semi-realistic
interpretation, as we have found possible for most of Hesse's
stories and novels up to *Knulp*. One can, of course, discern
personal traits in some of the characters of his dream world,
and Iris in particular has been interpreted as a poetic portrait
of his wife Maria. But all such interpretations overlook Hesse's
essential departure from Realism which takes place during
these years. The poet himself was conscious of it and signified
it by publishing his next novel *Demian* (1919) under the
pseudonym Emil Sinclair. He thus indicated a complete break

with his poetic past. (Isaac von Sinclair was the name of the lonely Hölderlin's most faithful friend.) Naturally, the pseudonym was soon found out, and Hesse had to give it up; but by that time it had served its purpose of shielding the poetic butterfly during its vulnerable chrysalid state.

The events and characters in *Demian* are symbolic experiences of the soldier Emil Sinclair who is searching for his integrated self. Sinclair, unlike his artistic predecessors, no longer wants to escape, but strives to accept life. He tries "to give life to that which wanted to come out of me by its own force" (III, 101). In his quest for his self he first returns to his childhood. Soon its protecting warmth is destroyed by the discovery of an outside world of violence and danger under the influence of Franz Kromer, a boy from the other side of the tracks. Sinclair himself for a while shares in Kromer's values and becomes a petty thief.

From this situation Sinclair is rescued by Demian, an older and more mature schoolmate. (The name is a distortion of the Greek *Daimon*, "demon," also "fate" and "conscience," and was found by Hesse in a dream.) While Kromer is actually introduced as Sinclair's base "shadow" (III, 129), Demian is his psychopompos and can set the negative forces into their proper perspective. He frees Sinclair from his shadow and becomes his intimate friend. Sinclair learns to appreciate the strong mentality of Demian, who is capable of thought transference and whose own thoughts go far beyond the platitudes of his teachers and his pastor. After a confirmation class Demian submits a spirited plea in favor of Cain. According to him, Cain did not commit murder but was blackballed because of his independent mind. This suggests a study of the Gnostic sects who worshipped the creative force, which they named Abraxas.

Demian uses this concept of Abraxas to instill in Sinclair an awareness of evil as a constituent part of the world and not as a mere outside force. We are all marked men like Cain, claims Demian, and Sinclair should therefore accept evil and no longer indulge in self-righteousness. He should no longer be afraid of the invisible divinity beyond bourgeois good and evil.

Sinclair first had to give up childlike innocence. Then he passed through a period where he could hope to become saved

by a fixed system of moral vaules. He had to learn that there is
no such salvation, as the good in man is inextricably intertwined
with the evil. Now he must reach the third stage where he accepts God who is sending both good and evil and yet is meaningful in his own, inscrutable way.

The path to such an acceptance is beset with pitfalls.
Sinclair revolts against Demian and for a while becomes a
wastrel. But then he confronts his deeper and purer self in the
figure of a lovely girl whom he never meets in person. This
"Beatrice," as he calls her, saves him from the loss of his artistic
abilities. He turns from his wasteful habits and begins to sketch
her. As he draws, he recognizes himself in her and is able to
design a better image of his self.

Another of Sinclair's pictures is that of a sparrow hawk
breaking out of its shell. (At this point it should be remembered
that Jungian practice encourages the patient to draw pictures
in order to make him face his subconscious images.) Sinclair
has reproduced this particular picture from memory, and it
copies an escutcheon over the door of his parents' home to which
Demian has once called his attention. In an unexplained manner Demian had inserted a note into Sinclair's notebook: "The
bird is fighting to break the egg. The egg is the world. He who
wants to be born, must destroy a world. The bird is flying to
God. The God's name is Abraxas" (III, 185).

In his "flight" toward Abraxas, Sinclair meets a second
guide in the person of the organist Pistorius, whose acquaintance
he has made in a tavern where Pistorius is drinking to forget his
sorrow at being an outcast and a seer. Pistorius encourages Sinclair in his restless pursuit of his true self, and the latter learns
his lesson well. He now draws a picture of a woman he has seen
in his dreams. The painting assumes the features of Sinclair's
mother, but again, she actually represents his deepest unconscious, with which Sinclair must identify himself. Significantly,
after Sinclair's evocation of his dream image Pistorius can no
longer help his charge and drops out of the picture. He has
represented the psychoanalytic physician whom the patient must
finally reject, in order to become independent and be cured.

The cure is symbolized by Sinclair's meeting with Demian's
mother. In a university town he again comes across Demian,

who takes his friend home to his mother. Gossip has her living
in incest with her son—a poetic transcription of her true character as a part of a mandala. The trio is united in the vision of a
new Europe, a future world in which people who have forged
their true personalities will emerge as leaders of a new humanity.
Sinclair regrets only that he cannot win Frau Eva for himself.
She tells him that she will come to him when his want of her
is strong enough to draw her to him.

One night Sinclair marshals all his strength to call her.
But instead, Demian enters with the news that the first world
war has broken out. The two young men become soldiers, because as such they can help to sweep away the insincere bourgeois world and put the dynamic civilization of the future in its
place. Since they move under the sign of Abraxas, the new
world will of course not be traditionally humanistic.

The two friends are separated by the war and for the last
time find each other again side by side in a hospital. Demian
dies from his wounds, but before his death gives Sinclair a last
kiss from Mother Eve, i.e., Sinclair becomes united with his
real self. The latter looks into his soul and sees his "own image
that now is entirely the likeness of him, my friend and mentor"
(III, 257).

The basic theme of the book is the emergence of Sinclair's
integrated self from his earlier schizoid separation into Demian
and the conventional Sinclair. To be sure, the ultimate integration—the union with Demian's mother—is never attained.
But it is at least visualized.

According to Jung, Christianity is a schizophrenic mascu-
line religion, a theory which fitted in nicely with Hesse's basic
aversion to orthodoxy. Abraxas is no longer a Father God, but
represents the invisible divinity with which *Unio mystica* is
sought. The name Abraxas is of course of Gnostic origin and as
such is a vulnerable concept. Hesse himself later called the
Gnostic elements of the story superficial. But the concept meant
a significant move away from the image of a so-called "good"
Father God in constant conflict with a "bad" world. This image
in popular forms of Christianity often amounted to a Mani-
chean dualism, where God and Satan contended for the
world.

In his quest for a more universal God, Hesse could appear temporarily as an advocate of Satan. In certain *Demian* passages he could actually speak out in favor of the devil's worship of sex, by which, after all, the world is perpetuated (III, 156; 188–189). But it would be utterly false to accuse Hesse of immorality. The recognition of man's suppressed desires is merely a necessary condition for their reshaping into meaningful drives. In the period when he was writing *Peter Camenzind*, Hesse still hoped to reach salvation by withdrawing from a hostile "world" into a Franciscan communion with nature. Now he was actively fighting for self-realization within as well as without himself. This meaning was conveyed not too clearly by the taking up of arms by Sinclair and Demian. Although this looked like an affirmation of war, it had only symbolical meaning for a convinced pacifist like Hesse. It was intended to signify the reshaping of the world by the spirit: "The world that exists wants to perish, and it will perish" (III, 228).

Stylistically, *Demian* signaled Hesse's definite break with his early regionalism and Impressionism. To be sure, his new style still preserved some realistic elements. Kromer, Demian, Pistorius, and even Demian's mother are entirely possible in real life and behave like human beings. But for Sinclair they represent archetypal experiences in his struggle for integration. They hold one meaning as persons of real life and another as archetypes of Sinclair's psychological world. The proper name for such a contrapuntal style would be Surrealism, if by Surrealism is meant the employing of real objects to express nonobjective experiences. In Hesse's case one can see the affinity of this style to Romanticism. In fact it can be traced directly to Novalis and Jean Paul (who must here be covered by a term somewhat incongruous for his peculiarity).

The stories of E. T. A. Hoffmann and Clemens Brentano would be other examples of this early use of reality as a foil for nonobjective experiences. Some of Hesse's symbols, e.g., the sparrow hawk breaking out of an eggshell, were taken from the Romantic philosopher Bachofen. In his main work, *Das Mutterrecht* (The Maternal Law, 1861), Bachofen had attempted to prove the existence of a maternal culture at the beginning of occidental civilization. His proofs had been certain motifs from archaic Greek and Roman grave sculptures, and such a motif was the sparrow hawk breaking out of an eggshell.

From *Demian* to *The Bead Game* Hesse continuously enhanced his style, and it was only in minor essays and autobiographical reminiscences that he again deserted it for pure Realism. One can, of course, discern variations in his surrealistic approach. While the style of *Narcissus and Goldmund* may be compared to the painting styles of Ernst Kirchner or Max Beckmann, the style of *Steppenwolf* and of *The Journey to the East* may remind one of Paul Klee or Marc Chagall. In any case we face here a world which is not fully obeying the laws of reality, but is rather moving in its own magic orbits. Whenever Hesse wanted to describe his vocation from this time on, he introduced himself as a "magician."

His new surrealistic style held great appeal for the young generation that had preceded or was living through World War I. For the second time since *Peter Camenzind* and *Under the Wheel*, Hesse found himself in the forefront of the literary wave. Although he was connected with no group or school of writers and avoided literary cliques, his *Demian* became a favorite among intellectuals. It was classed with other contemporary productions which also rejected the world of the father and tried to find a home in the creative world of the mother, like Walter Hasenclever's drama *Der Sohn* (The Son, 1914) or Fritz von Unruh's play *Ein Geschlecht* (A Generation, 1916). A great wave of religious sentiment also swept in with this so-called expressionism.

Unfortunately the enthusiasm for *Demian* did not last, and German youth did not follow its admonitions. Other ideas and other leaders competed for its soul, and it became hostile to self-analysis. But Hesse's personal isolation was now broken, at least so far as the literary public and the booksellers were concerned. He could face the future with greater confidence.

6 · A New Beginning

THE ENDING of *Demian* has a Nietzschean ring. Sinclair's acceptance of the breakdown of bourgeois civilization reminds one
of Nietzsche's *amor fati*, and his taking up of arms represents a
Nietzschean act of defiance. An essay published before *Demian*
bore the characteristic title *Eigensinn* (1918; VII, 197–200),
"defiant individualism." Like *Demian*, this essay appeared under
the pseudonym "Emil Sinclair." No author except an anonymous
"German" was named for the pamphlet *Zarathustra's Return*
(*Zarathustras Wiederkehr*, 1919; VII, 200–230). It was written
in three days and three nights during January 1919, and was
addressed to German youth, whom Zarathustra rebuked for their
expectation of outside help and advice. Through the mouth of
Zarathustra, Hesse argued that the fatal prewar mistake of many
Germans was their dependence on material comforts and their
hunger for living space.

Now that the operatic splendor of the Wilhelmine era had
yielded to lustreless reality, Hesse implored German youth to
accept the defeat of the Reich and to help build a new, demo-
cratic Germany. He told them they should recognize themselves
for what they were—average people with many faults and perhaps a few virtues. Rather than try to improve the world, they
should try to cure themselves. Certainly they were now suffering;
but they must recognize suffering as a constituent part of life
and learn to live with it instead of opposing it. "From suffering
comes strength, from suffering comes health" (VII, 213). It is
a childish wish to want to change one's fate; the emperors and

generals have often tried to do so, but in vain. But fate only tastes bitter so long as one opposes it as something hostile which comes from the outside. Once one accepts it, it becomes bearable.

From October 1919 to December 1922 Hesse sought to promulgate such thoughts through the monthly *Vivos Voco*, which he edited in collaboration with Richard Woltereck. (The title of the magazine was taken from a Latin inscription on the bell which Friedrich Schiller had described in his *Lay of the Bell*: "I am calling the living.") After 1922 Hesse limited his contribution to reviews. In a way *Vivos Voco* continued its common efforts for the prisoners of war, for the net income from the magazine was assigned to the relief work for German children, who still suffered from the allied food blockade.

One particularly ugly way of putting the blame on others, the way of virulent anti-Semitism, was castigated by Hesse as early as 1922. Even in 1924 he had not yet given up hope that in due course of time his nation would start a soul-searching process,

. . . not the whole nation, but many wide-awake and responsible individuals, and would replace in a thousand hearts the complaints and scoldings about the bad war and the bad peace and the bad revolution by the question: "In what way have I myself shared in the guilt? And how can I again become innocent?" For at any time one can again become innocent by realizing one's guilt and accepting its implications instead of seeking the blame in others (*Neue Rundschau*, 1924, p. 104).

Yet Hesse's hope for a German return to sanity could not be sustained indefinitely. Though the *Zarathustra* essay was published in part in the *Wandervögel* magazine *Freideutsche Jugend* (1919), only a few young idealists heeded its warning, and Hesse increasingly became a lone voice in the wilderness. Not only Germany, but the whole of Europe, was running away from Nietzsche's rationalism and emphatic responsibility and embracing an irrational emotionalism. The idol of this modern Europe was the Russian character as portrayed by Dostoevski.

Hesse warned against the Russian idol in the essay *The Brothers Karamasoff or the End of Europe (Die Brüder Kara-*

masoff oder der Untergang Europas, 1920; VII, 161–178). For
this Russian man was a chaotic drifter without clear orientation.

The Russian man, the Karamasoff, is at once a murderer and a
judge, at once most brutal and most tender, he is the most consistent egotist to the same degree as he is a hero of the most abject
self-sacrifice. He cannot be understood from an avowedly European
moral, ethical, and dogmatic point of view. In this man's soul
good and bad, God and Satan dwell next to each other" (VII, 165).
[But] . . . already half of Europe, at least half of Eastern Europe,
is on its way to chaos, is skirting the abyss in a holy, intoxicated
frenzy, and is singing drunken paeans like Dmitri Karamasoff. These
songs are insulting the bourgeois whom they move to painful
laughter. The saint and the seer are moved to tears (VII, 178).

Naturally Hesse was thinking of the Russian revolution,
which had broken out in 1917, but he knew also that its cruelties
were only the most radical expression of a general phenomenon.
There were numerous people who led an irreproachable family
life while at the same time forming efficient parts of an unfeel-
ing technical civilization. (It is worthy of notice that the essay
on Dostoevski was written before the publication of Oswald
Spengler's *Decline of the West* [1918], which was also skeptical
of the moral tenor of the age.)

Dostoevski himself naturally did not set up the Karamazoff
as an ideal. He was a Greek Orthodox Christian and introduced
his characters as self-accusers and confessors, baring their souls
to their last sinful depths. For the Russian writer no man was
wholly just. All were seed of the devil, and every man had to
accept his share in mankind's total guilt. This was a gospel
compatible with the doctrines of modern psychoanalysis, and
Hesse was to follow it eventually in *Steppenwolf*. But for the
time being, Nietzsche forbade him to wallow in self-accusation.
He could not, however, forever shake off the feelings of hope-
lessness and progressive doom, and the martial notes of *Demian*
and of *Zarathustra's Return* were not repeated.

In 1920 Hesse published three new tales under the common
title *Klingsor's Last Summer*. The first, *Kinderseele* (Childhood), was written in 1918 and suggested the Nietzschean solution of *Demian*. It re-created one of those fateful moments of
childhood when obedience to parental commandments is no

longer taken on trust and the first thought of evil enters the innocent mind. It also portrayed the first painful assertion of coming independence. The story was the last one to be preoccupied with Hesse's own childhood. After *Kinderseele*, his attention was wholly devoted to problems of maturity.

However, *Klein and Wagner* (1919–1920; III, 466–554), the second story, avoids a Nietzschean assertion. It tells the story of a man who can cope neither with the exigencies of his former bourgeois existence nor with the newly awakened sensuousness of his subconscious, and in the end simply gives up the struggle in Schopenhauerean despair. Klein starts out as a respectable bank employee and family man. But he is unable to keep up his middle-class pretensions without embezzling money and forging passports. Finally he runs away from his responsibilities and tries to start a new life. He lets himself be guided by the suppressed demon in his soul, by the evil *anima*. His secret idol becomes the murderer Wagner, a South German school teacher who ruthlessly slaughtered his whole family and then killed himself.

When Klein arrives in a small Italian lakeside resort, he pays for everything with embezzled money. He has an adventure with an innkeeper's wife, who has been deserted by her husband. Then he starts a stormy affair with the dancer Teresina. After one particularly violent scene, Klein is seized by the desire to murder Teresina and immediately sets out to execute his plan. But he is unable to find a knife and therefore runs away.

At the shore of the lake he comes across a boat, which he enters and pushes into the water. When it has drifted far enough, Klein climbs overboard and lets himself fall. He cannot really face himself in the way that *Demian* espoused Nietzschean self-knowledge. Klein is too weak to lead a completely asocial life, and he is likewise unable to resume his former bourgeois existence. So he chooses the path of least resistance and gives himself up. This avoidance of a decision fills his soul with a vision of infinite bliss. He has annihilated his unsatisfactory personality and become united with the universe, of which he has been but one fleeting moment. Extinguishing himself, Klein can submerge in God, whose praise is his ultimate utterance.

The end of Hesse's story is more convincing than the end

of Georg Kaiser's drama *From Morn to Midnight* (1916), which treated the same subject but failed to imbue its last scene with life. The conversion of Kaiser's cashier affects the reader as a cheap theatrical trick.

This giving up of oneself, this "letting oneself fall," is also the predominant theme of *Klingsor's Last Summer* (*Klingsors letzter Sommer*, 1919), the third story of the book. The title itself indicates that self-abandonment is stressed, for "last" here means "ultimate, final, suicidal." In the beginning of the story it is stated soberly that Klingsor has died, although the narrator mentions at the same time that his life has become surrounded by myths. Actually, only the intoxicated and exuberant Klingsor is symbolically rejected at the end, and a tame and conventional contemporary emerges. This solution is highly ironical. In truth, it is no solution at all. Klingsor's life is an attempt to live in both worlds—in the untamed world of the senses and the ordinary world of contemporary civilization. The result is little more than a passing escapade.

On the surface, Klingsor's story is merely trying to capture the exceptional Ticino summer of 1919. But this summer stands for the totality of sensual existence; a totality exhilarating by its vitality and continuously succumbing to death and decay at the same time. Death is always hovering before Klingsor's mind and is tinging his bursts of uninhibited self-enjoyment with melancholy. "Klingsor was looking at the black doors. Death stood outside. He saw him standing. He smelled death like one smells rain drops in the scattered leaves of the highway" (III, 597). Decline and downfall are also new birth and resurrection: every end is a beginning. Here, Hesse is taking leave of the setting sun of nineteenth-century Europe, from the friendly evening calm of Keller's *Seldwyla* stories, and starting out in a new, violent world of inner disturbances and searing sincerity. There is in the story all the melancholy of decay and dying, and all the explosiveness of sensuous passion and intoxication.

Klingsor is painting "free paraphrases of reality" (III, 555) in very few colors; but these colors are uncommonly bright. He is absorbed in the profound drinking songs of his favorite poet Li Tai Po, and often calls himself Li Tai Po. Klingsor flirts with chaos. He is acutely touched by every longing, sick with every vice, enthusiastically inspired by the knowledge of his own demise, prepared for every progress, ripe for every reaction, wholly glow and wholly lassitude, dedicated to fate and pain like the drug addict to poison, lonely, caved in, ancient, Faust as well as Karamasoff, animal as well as wise man, wholly bore, wholly without ambition, wholly naked, full of childish fear of death and full of tired readiness to die (III, 610–611).

Klingsor's life pulsates between Dionysian abandon and continuous awareness of death, between searing passion and contemplative meditation. He drinks the cups of wine and of love in great gulps, yet he knows that this episode will not last forever. Some day in the future the wind will rustle over his grave. But he will not be alone. The "eternal mother" will then bend over him, she who, like Goethe's "Mothers" in *Faust*, symbolizes the immortal mainspring of ever-recurring life in the midst of the perishable world. She also symbolizes Hesse's resignation to his fate. Yet there is not only Goethe in his mind, but also Nietzsche. ("Louis the Cruel" is a Nietzschean term.)

In conformity with the abandoned mood, the landscape setting is transformed into a magic unreality.

Beneath him descended down into dizzying depths the old terrace garden, a thicket of ample tree tops—palms, cedars, chestnuts, Judas trees, red beeches, eucalyptus—in dark shadows intertwined with climbers, lianas, glycinias. Over the black trees lay the shine of the pale, big, tinny reflecting leaves of the summer magnolias, amongst them enormous, snow-white blossoms, half opened, big like human heads, pale like the moon and like ivory, from which a peculiarly penetrating and enervating fragrance drifted over. Music came from an undetermined distance, flying on tired wings, perhaps from a guitar, perhaps from a piano, one could not make it out. In the poultry yards there suddenly shrieked a peacock two or three times and tore the forest night with the short, evil, and wooden sound of his pained voice, as if all the sufferings of the animal world sounded shrilly from primeval depths. Starlight was flowing through the valley, a white, tall, deserted chapel peaked like old magic from the infinite forest. The lake, the mountains, and the sky intermingled in the distance (III, 556–557).

Klingsor completely forgets himself in these nightly musings, and his friend Louis the Cruel tries in vain to induce him to face reality. For Klingsor, art is not merely a substitute for sensuality; he does not pain for want of something better. In a painting by Luigi (i.e., Louis), he loves most of all a small spot taken up by a little flag. "In this small, stupid, pink flag is all the woe and all the resignation of the world, and also all the good laughter over the woe and the resignation" (III, 565). The spiritual and the sensual belong together and must not be separated.

Klingsor embraces life in all its aspects, be they ever so fleeting and momentary. We partake with him in a mountain climb to Monte Gennaro; in the flights of his fancy to Africa and Nagasaki, to India and to the South Seas; in his wining and dining with his friends in the beautiful July nights. And amid all these elations, Klingsor is changing. He savors the melancholy of the change from life to death and back again to new birth. He sends one of his realistic paintings to Louis the Cruel and a drinking song to his other friend Hermann the poet written in the manner of Tu Fu:

Vieles tat und erlitt ich,	I did and I suffered many things,
Wandrer auf langem Weg.	a wanderer on a long road.
Nun am Abend sitz ich,	Now I sit in the evening,
trinke und warte bang,	drink and wait in fear,
Bis die blitzende Sichel	Until the sparkling scythe
Mir das Haupt vom zuckenden	Shall sever my head from my
Herzen trennt.	beating heart.

(III, 608).

In the end he tries to encompass his whole personality by assembling all his faces in a self-portrait. He neither wants to escape from reality into the realm of pure fancy, nor resign to it in the manner of Louis the Cruel, who professes to see no sense in anything and has succumbed to the lure of the material. But the attempted integration of both attitudes is unsuccessful.

At the end of these whipped-up days he put the finished picture into the unused, empty kitchen and locked it up. He never showed the picture to anyone. Then he took Veronal and slept for a whole day and a whole night. Afterwards he washed and shaved, put on new underwear and new clothing, went to town and bought fruit and cigarettes, as a present for Gina (II, 614).

To understand *Klingsor's Last Summer,* one must read a great deal between the lines. Hesse does not make it easy for the reader in this most personal of his books. At the same time

he is filling our minds with unforgettable images. The name of
Klingsor is taken from the unfinished novel *Heinrich von Ofterdingen* by Novalis, who had found it in Wolfram von Eschenbach's *Parzival* as the name of a powerful magician. (Because of
Hesse's dislike for Wagner [cf. II, 515; III, 483; VII, 225] it
is not likely that Klingsor's name was taken from *Parsifal*.)
Hesse frequently described his view of the world as magical,
and he liked to designate his own calling as that of a magician.
One might therefore be tempted to call Klingsor a self-portrait,
if Klingsor did not have so many different faces. Hermann the
poet, who calls himself Tu Fu, is intended as a self-portrait of
Hesse. Louis the Cruel is a parody of the painter Louis Moilliet,
while the Armenian magician is a mask for the architect Josef
Englert. Finally, Hesse brought Ruth Wenger into this story.
(Half a decade later she became his second wife.) She appears
as the queen of the mountains from the parrot house in Corona.
Yet all of these people are changed and transformed; their
portraits emerge as expressionistic explosions. The book is in
no way a simple diary.

Expressionism is of course a vague term to describe Hesse's
style in *Klingsor's Last Summer*. The word has served as a
catchall for the leading German writers who emerged in the
second and third decades of the twentieth century. In the case
of *Klingsor*, the term refers to a purposely exaggerated and exuberant style which indulges in broad, violent splashes of color
and recklessly ecstatic moods.

This style, however, was new only on the surface. In 1899,
An Hour Beyond Midnight had contained night scenes in which
red fires burned in stone bowls, the heavy night air carried the
great rhythm of the distant sea; and the narrator sang bewitch-
ing, melancholy songs to the accompaniment of a guitar (I, 17).
Already in this early book there was a tale of a secret park where
strange deer and colorful, foreign birds were hidden, and a
century-old artificial wilderness full of rare flowers surrounded
a hunting lodge filled with memories of sinful revelries (I, 37).
Such heady *Jugendstil* dreams now became the substance of
Klingsor's Last Summer. At times its style became unmistakably
turgid. It must have appeared so even to Hesse, since he never
resumed this exaggerated manner again.

Yet the best passages of *Klingsor* excel in a certain musical quality. Many sentences start with a bright fanfare and end in a series of notes quickly diminishing in intensity: "A tiny village lay on the mountain crest: a manorial estate with a small residential house, four or five other houses, stone-houses, painted blue and pinkish, a chapel, a well, cherry trees" (III, 574). The rhythm of such sentences is strong and frequently triadic: "At the top was a monument, a lonely baroque bust stood there, in Wallenstein's costume, with locks, with a wavy goatee" (III, 575). The triadic structure can also consist of long, artfully sustained clauses united in a single sentence: "Klingsor loved old pictures when he hit upon them without searching, he loved such frescoes, he loved the return of these beautiful works to dust and earth" (III, 575). But there are also sentences with only two clauses, each accented in the beginning and then subsiding into artful calmness: "Female slaves were crouching on the steps at her feet, the many-hued parrot flew screeching on the shoulder of his mistress" (III, 577).

A characteristic element of style in *Klingsor's Last Summer* is its richness of color, which has already been demonstarted in the previous quotations. Sensitivity to color was also evident in many passages of *An Hour Beyond Midnight* and *Hermann Lauscher* (1901), but now it is carefully trained and nurtured. This is the result of Hesse's sudden discovery, at the age of forty, of a certain affinity to painting. He found a new creative outlet for his emotions in this pastime, which he pursued as a dilettante.

With a small folding-chair, a box of water colors, and a block of drawing paper, he roamed over the Collina d'Oro, sketching its hills, its trees, its houses, its chapels, and its churches; playing a distracting and yet satisfying game with shapes and colors. Hesse found that painting made him more patient and more serene. It could change reality, make houses laugh or weep, give face and wings to trees. The little palette of the hobbyist became an arsenal. The accent was on color; contour was unimportant.

This technique shows a certain relation to the painters' group known as the *Blue Riders*, of which Paul Klee was co-founder. Louis Moilliet had told Hesse a great deal about Klee, and his other friend Ernst Morgenthaler for a time was a Klee disciple. With them, painting became a dramatic action as it did for Wassily Kandinsky. Colors behaved almost as independent creatures—now combining and running together, now waging wars against each other. Ochre, Neapolitan yellow, English red, white, very bright madder, Parisian blue, cinnabar were favorite actors in a never-ending game. And all meant something. "Purple was denial of death, cinnabar was scornful derision of decay" (III, 589).

At times Hesse toyed with the thought of deserting literature and devoting his life to painting. Some later books like *Wanderung* ("Hikings," 1920) and *Piktors Verwandlungen* ("Pictor's Many Faces," published in facsimile in 1925) became syntheses of paintings, lyrics, and prose. They remind one at times of Klee. These books were sold as illustrated manuscripts to collectors and helped Hesse to overcome the losses caused by the difficult years of German inflation. It should be noted also that *Klingsor's Last Summer* could never have been written without the poet's personal essay in painting. Inspiration came also from the beauty of a southern landscape.

In 1919 Hesse settled in a part of Switzerland far removed from Germany. After his wife Maria's dismissal from the mental institution, continuation of the marriage had proved impossible, and the poet found himself alone in a deserted house. The children were living in boarding schools or with friends. Hesse realized that it was no longer possible to stay in Bern and began looking for a new home in the Italian-speaking Ticino area of southern Switzerland. Its landscape corresponded more closely to the poet's changed state of mind than did the idyllic peace of Lake Constance or the staid atmosphere of Bern. Here was a combination of exotic exuberance and classic moderation; of subtropical vegetation and orderly gardening; of the beauty of adventure and the memory of childhood.

Hesse first tried Minusio near Locarno, then Sorengo, and finally rented the Casa Camuzzi in Montagnola near Lugano, an odd nineteenth-century imitation of a baroque hunting castle. Here the poet remained, with only occasional brief excursions, for the rest of his life.

The subtropical Montagnola landscape and the Italian

linguistic climate enabled Hesse to keep aloof from literary circles and pursue his inner quest without hindrance. He seldom left the Casa Camuzzi and virtually lived the life of a hermit. To be sure, he gave readings from his poetry in St. Gallen, in Bern, and in Zurich. He visited Ruth Wenger and her family and C. G. Jung. But for practical reasons he could not indulge in the luxury of many trips. The increasing inflation of the mark was reducing his German income to a trickle, and he had to borrow occasionally from Swiss friends. The poet could describe himself as almost a derelict, who wore shabby suits and lived on rice and macaroni and on chestnuts gathered in the woods.

Yet this shabby hermit made rapid inner progress. *Klingsor* was the last story which ended without providing a real solution. In his next work, *Siddhartha*, Hesse achieved a quite different meaning, although even this story did not provide his final answer to the problem of existence.

7 · The Turn Inward

Demian as well as *Klingsor's Last Summer* already had visualized an ironical acceptance of the world as a possible solution for the problem of human existence. Yet because of their contemporary connotations both stories were open to misunderstanding. It was not conformity that Hesse was advocating, but a reshaping of the world from within. *The Turn Inward* (*Der Weg nach Innen*) was the common title chosen by him, in 1931, when he brought *Siddhartha* and *Klingsor's Last Summer* together under the same cover. The "turn inward" was meant to be described in both *Demian* and *Klingsor*.

For the reader of *Siddhartha* (1922) no further misunderstanding was possible. The Indian locale at once removed Hesse from contemporary European realities and forced him to come to grips with the existential problem. The story also made Hesse's message universal by no longer addressing itself to occidentals only.

Siddhartha is based on the life of Buddha. (Siddhartha was Buddha's original name and means the man who is on the right road.) But the interpretation of Buddha's life is by no means traditional, and the India of Siddhartha is far removed from the reality Hesse experienced in 1911. The poet has concentrated on the "subterranean, timeless world of spiritual values" (III, 857).

The son of a Brahmin, Siddhartha, at first seems content to follow the pious Hindu's path to salvation through chastity, which is here stressed in a way comparable to Protestant Pietism. However, he becomes aware that the precepts of his parents and tutors do not fit his spiritual needs, and he decides to leave home to seek his own salvation. With his friend Govinda he joins the Samanas, an ascetic sect of beggars. Both learn to restrain their impulses and to concentrate on the spirit which is innate in man and is united with the spirit of the universe. Such concentration is achieved by the practice of Yoga.

After a time, however, Yoga no longer yields true satisfaction. It is merely a step toward fulfillment; it does not represent the whole way. Siddhartha feels that trust in detailed moral prescription leads only to despair. Man can never hope for salvation by external works; he must give up his self-righteousness. It is useless to starve and maim oneself in order to find the secret behind the fragments of life. The youth therefore sets out to live a real life in the spirit—a life in Atman.

Now, Siddhartha studies the teachings of Gotama Buddha and strives "to die away from himself, to be an ego no longer, . . . to be open to the miracle in a selfless spirit" (III, 626). He learns that Buddha teaches his disciples to control their senses without extinguishing them, promising salvation in the Nirvana. Govinda becomes a Buddhistic monk, but Siddhartha cannot accept the whole doctrine. To him real experience is more revealing than all the formal doctrines of religion, including the concept of Nirvana.

Siddhartha enters the world of Samsara, the disturbing cycle of earthly happenings. As the lover of the courtesan Kamala he becomes a rich merchant, a gambler, and a drinker. But this type of life proves to be empty, since it is lived in the fearful world of man's fiendish cruelty and lust of evil. A disillusioned Siddhartha leaves his wealth behind and sets out to drown himself in the river. At this point Klein's solution looms as a possibility. But Siddhartha happens to meet the ferryman Vasudeva and is taught by him to "sleep on the wave," i.e., to have confidence in life and to be in harmony with nature.

This "sleep on the wave" overcomes time, which already for Klingsor was a deception. "Was not all suffering time, was not all self-vexation and fear time, did not everything hostile and heavy in the world disappear and was overcome, as soon as one had conquered time, as soon as one became able to extin-

guish time?" (III, 698). Life through this act of time-negation
opens up and gains a fourth dimension.

Siddhartha has a momentary vision of Brahma, the absolute divinity behind all worldly deceptions. He pronounces the
sacred syllable "Om" and anticipates the life of mystic intuition, the *via illuminativa*. But he has not yet followed the way of
purification, the *via purgativa*, to the end. He has merely taken
the first step by giving up his luxurious existence and living
a simple life of solitude.

Kamala brings him a son she has borne him, and turns aside
to die. Siddhartha now has to take care of his son. The son,
however, does not understand his father and eventually runs
back to the city. Siddhartha is heartbroken, but Vasudeva reminds him that his own father had the same experience when
Siddhartha left home.

Now the pilgrim is ready to enter the *via illuminativa*. He
resigns from Samsara completely and, after Vasudeva's death,
himself becomes the ferryman. He lives beside the river and
consoles all travelers. Govinda, who comes to visit him, believes
Siddhartha to be a saint. He is taught by Siddhartha the unity
of life, the unity of night and day, of *I* and *thou*, of poverty and
affluence, of flesh and spirit. Siddhartha tells him that only by
living a life of both the spirit and the senses will he gain peace.

The new ferryman's wisdom has been gained from the
river. The river has become his teacher and the voice of life,
which is continuously changing. Siddhartha is not one of those
mystics who shut out the world by withdrawing into their selves.
His mysticism is immersion into life. He aims, like Friedrich
Schleiermacher, "in the midst of final life to become one with
the infinite and to be eternal in a moment" (*Speeches on Religion*, 1799). This immersion into life enables Siddhartha to
shed great parts of his individuality and to find inner freedom.

The first stage of his way to freedom had been innocence.
The second stage was the observation of a system of moral
prescriptions in the certain hope of reaching salvation. The
third stage was characterized by the discovery of ineradicable
evil and the consequent abandonment of all hope. The fourth
stage is reached by the acceptance of evil and the resumption of

ordained tasks. Only now, when justification is left to the God-head, does the real path to salvation, the *via unitiva*, lie open. Siddhartha can aspire to vedantic identity mysticism. To be sure, complete identity with the all-embracing divinity is open to him as little as to other men. But he can live within the higher divinity.

It must be seen clearly that this is a continuation of Hesse's early theopanism and not simply "pantheism." God *is* here the cosmos and expresses himself by it; the cosmos has no separate existence without him or within him. The central idea of this theopanism is unity. In the vision transferred to him by Siddhartha, Govinda no longer sees the face of his friend Siddhartha, but a continuous stream of faces "which all came and disappeared and yet all seemed to be there at the same time, which all continually changed and renewed themselves and which were yet all Siddhartha" (III, 731). They represent all ages and sexes; they change into the faces of animals and gods. Yet there hovers above this welter of passing forms the smile of unity, "this smile of simultaneousness over thousands of births and deaths," which is also the "thousand-fold smile of Gotama, the Buddha" (III, 732). Before this smile Govinda is "overwhelmed by a feeling of great love, of the most humble veneration" (III, 733).

There is here a certain stressing of passivity, and the story can almost be interpreted as an illustration of Hinayana Buddhism or of the Upanishad's way to salvation. It seems to resume Klein's and Klingsor's solution on a higher level. But there is more to it than passivity. Siddhartha has not become a monk, but a ferryman; he has shown active concern for the other travelers and for Govinda, as well as for his son.

Despite the Eastern coloration, the message of *Siddhartha* is Christian, even Protestant Christian, not Asiatic. Mystic union in the last instance means a loving embrace of the world. One could justifiably quote Christ's pronouncement that "God is not the God of the dead, but of the living" (Matth. 23:32). Hesse aims at a synthesis of Eastern and Christian thought. Western intellectual arrogance and impatience is tempered by Eastern contemplation and humility. Eastern mysticism is expressed in a Western concern for the world's creatures. Of course, this concern is not to be equated with the Platonic *eros* where the love of the beautiful form leads back to the original idea as the true basis of reality. On the contrary, the way here leads *from* the union with the transcendental *to* beauty as an expression and metaphor of God.

Potentially all things participate in God, and the more man succeeds in changing these potentialities into actualities, the more he realizes himself and participates in divine love. Love for one's neighbor and love for the world are ways to self-realization. Siddhartha's experience of mystic union does not lead to spiritual aloofness, for man can never wholly divest himself of the earth, he is "never wholly saint, nor is he ever wholly sinner" (III, 725). Siddhartha's way leads to humble, Christian charity. In all his awareness of the infinite realm of God and the universe, he remains a simple ferryman and farmer.

Still we must not forget that the book is a work of art, and not a philosophical treatise. Its ideas are implicit; they are never expressed outright. The charm of *Siddhartha* lies in its unforgettable images. The god-seeker's childhood among the Brahmins, his ceaseless ascetic roamings with the Samanas, his mad worldly exploits with Kamala, and finally his meeting with Vasudeva and his life as his disciple, are all parts of a closely interwoven tapestry. They are far from being flowery transcriptions of abstract formulas. A symbolic expression like "sleeping on the wave" is of unusual poetic depth. It is comparable to Goethe's description of poetry as "water shaped into a ball." The final meaning of *Siddhartha*, just as the ultimate meaning of life, defies philosophic definition and can be hinted at only by the poetic symbol. It remains forever closed to the literal mind unable to read between the lines.

In keeping with the introspective theme of the story, the technique of narration here is different from the one employed in *Klingsor's Last Summer*. The natural background of the two books is similar, but the perspective has changed. In *Klingsor's Last Summer*, the garden of the Casa Camuzzi became an overriding symphony of sound and color. Here it has taken on calm, restrained, and almost classic features. The exotic jungle of *Klingsor* has become the grove of contemplation, the Indian forest of sallows and fig trees and shadowy mangoes.

Everywhere the stress is on the essentials of the description, and these essentials are intensified by repetition and intensifying variation:

He however, Siddhartha, did not fashion joy for himself, he did not live for his pleasure. Walking on the rosy paths of the fig garden, sitting in the bluish shadow of the grove of contemplation, washing his limbs in daily ablutions, doing his sacrifices in the deep shadows of the mango forest, loved by all for the perfect grace of his gestures, and a joy for everybody, he yet bore no joy in his heart (III, 618).

The profuse orchestration of *Klingsor* is reduced to the measured rhythm of short, direct sentences, precisely balanced: "He came to the river, he asked the Old One to ferry him across, and when they left the boat on the other side, he said to the Old One: 'Much good you do to us monks and pilgrims. Many of us you have ferried across. Aren't you, ferryman, a seeker for the right path?'" (III, 722). With Hesse, all the images keep their full weight and can therefore be expressed in stark, even archaic, simplicity. His parallels are intensifications, not verbosities. Labored involutions are absent, but dependent clauses are not avoided: "The years passed by, and nobody counted them. Then monks came on a pilgrimage, disciples of Gotama, the Buddha, who asked to be ferried across the river, and who informed the ferryman that they were hurriedly walking back to their great teacher, for the news had spread that the sublime one was sick unto death and would soon die his last human death, in order to enter into salvation" (III, 700).

In these circumstantial clauses with their interruptions and their afterthoughts, the restlessness of the Buddhistic monks is aptly expressed, while Siddhartha himself gains peace by listening in silence to the river and remaining at his post. His calmness is described in simpler sentences, the repetition of which are slowly growing extensions of thought:

Siddhartha was listening. He now was nothing but a listener, wholly engrossed in listening, wholly emptied, wholly breathing in, he was feeling that he now had mastered listening to the end. He had often heard all this, these many voices in the river; today they sounded like new. He already could no longer differentiate between the many voices, between the happy ones and the weeping ones, between the childish and the manlike voices, they were all belonging together, the plaints of longing and the laughter of the sage, the shout of the irate and the moans of the dying man; they all were one, everything was interwoven and tied together, was intertwined a thousandfold. And everything together, all the voices, all the goals, all longing, all suffering, all good and evil, all this together was the world (III, 720).

As in *Klingsor*, the rhythm in *Siddhartha* is often triadic. "He felt a great desire to laugh, to laugh at himself, to laugh at this strange, foolish world" (III, 689). "Siddhartha felt what a great happiness it was to confess to such a listener, to sink into his heart one's own life, one's own strivings, one's own sufferings" (III, 696). Again there are sentences arranged in contrapuntal parallels: "Wonderful insight came to me through the teachings of the great Buddha, I felt the knowledge of the unity of the world circulate within me like my own blood. But I also had to leave again Buddha and the great knowledge" (III, 689).

Staccato passages of intensifying enumeration are scattered through the entire book. "The sun browned his light shoulders on the river bank, at bathing, at the holy ablutions, at the holy sacrifices. Shadow flowed into his black eyes in the mango grove, during his games, while his mother sang during the sacred sacrifices, during the teachings of his learned father, during the conversations of the wise men" (III, 617). At times this style assumes the character of a ritual chant. Its musical quality is unmistakable, but the music is more subdued than in *Klingsor*. Such a style does not represent the studied mannerism of artificial simplicity. It is rich enough in varitions to capture our undivided attention, and yet it is pure, as only the style of a master can be pure.

The highly spiritual view of the world presented in *Siddhartha* exercised its appeal on West and East alike. Hesse's book found recognition in Japan as well as in India itself. The Japanese translations put Hesse in the first place among all German authors whose works appeared in the East in translation, and lectures on the book were given at the Zen-Buddhistic university of Komadzawa in Tokyo. In India the book was translated into nine major dialects, and an Indian scholar praised *Siddhartha* as a proud tribute to the sons of India by one of the great contemporary spirits. He was amazed to find a European who had actually understood the spirit of the country.

For Western readers, *Siddhartha* climaxed centuries of effort to penetrate Eastern thought and religion and to understand that God had revealed himself to mankind in different ways. At the end of the nineteenth century it had become a common conviction of enlightened Easterners and Westerners alike that the Orient and the Occident could very well learn from each other. The seventeenth-century Jesuits had opened up the world of China to the European mind. About 1780 the great Sanskrit scholars had laid before it the world of India. The naval demonstration of Commodore Perry before Tokyo in 1854 had initiated an era of lively economic and cultural interchange between the West and the Far East, and had engendered an Eastern fashion among Western painters and decorators, poets and philosophers. Profound thinkers like Aldous Huxley and Romain Rolland found themselves obliged to justify the occidental, Christian attitude to the East and to accommodate the Western mind to profound Eastern insights. The West was reminded that it must give up its intellectual pride and admit the Eastern spirit of reverence.

For Hesse himself, the world of the East had been a living reality from his childhood. His trip to India, Malaya, and Sumatra had not even been necessary. At an early age he had realized the independence of the Orient and had begun to doubt the wisdom of the Christian missionary efforts. In the story *Robert Aghion* (1913; II, 355–394) he described the experiences of the first English missionary to India. Aghion had soon become convinced that it was presumptuous to take away their God from these strangers and in the end had succumbed to the lure of India. Like the author, Robert Aghion no longer felt certain of his mission and the superiority of his European ways.

At this point the poet's mind was refreshed by a study of oriental classics in excellent translations which, from 1890, had been brought out by far-sighted German publishers. These studies often included scholarly annotations and introductions. Previously, the oriental image of the German Romanticists had been based primarily on William Jones' translation of Kâlidâsa's

Sakuntala. Lao-tse had still been unknown to them. Even Schopenhauer had to be satisfied with Anquetil Duperron's translation of *Oupnekh' at* (1801), at that time the only Eastern work of consequence available. He did not know that the "divine" *Oupnekh' at* was a Persian, and therefore second-hand, extract from the original *Vedas.*

It was only at the end of the nineteenth century that Paul Deussen's translation of the *Upanishads* (1897) and Karl Eugen Neumann's rendering of the Buddhistic Canon made the documents of Indian religion available in the original. Neumann's *Dhammapada* came out in 1893; his *Last Days of Gotamo Buddho* (*Mahaparinibbana-Sutta*) in 1911. *Die chinesische Flöte,* Hans Bethge's free adaptation of Chinese poetry from English and French sources, appeared in 1907. Richard Wilhelm's *Tao-tê ching* was printed in 1911. It was part of his monumental translation of the Chinese classics, of which *I Ching* (1924) was to influence Hesse's thoughts profoundly. All of these translations enabled the nonlinguist to penetrate oriental thought to a degree unknown among older specialists.

The evidence of the Orient became so overwhelming that lesser spirits could give themselves Buddhistic and Confucian airs. This became fashionable in the nineteen-twenties, when World War I had so visibly demonstrated the breakdown of European culture. Now Max Dauthendey's, Karl Gjellerup's, and Waldemar Bonsels's stories from India and Malaya found an appreciative public, and Rudolf Steiner's anthroposophic movement was spawned by Indian thought. Count Hermann Keyserling's *Travel Diary of a Philosopher* (1919), with its more critical appreciation of Buddhistic thought, became a publisher's success. This was the climate of public opinion in which Hesse's own *Siddhartha* found a deeply gratifying echo.

Siddhartha was begun in 1919 and finished in 1922. The process of its gestation was interrupted by a period of one and a half years, while Hesse studied comparative religion and meditated closely on his subject. The first part of the novel was dedicated to Romain Rolland, the second to Wilhelm Gundert, Hesse's "Cousin from Japan." In the last years of the poet's life, Gundert's translation of the basic document of Zen Buddhism appeared, with an introduction by Hesse.

Still, the end of *Siddhartha* was clearly not Buddhistic, and its affirmative attitude toward life appeared to Western critics to be more Christian than Indian. This statement of course does not hold true when one has read the Brahmanistic *Bhagavad-Gita* (*The Song of the Lord*), where life pursued in a spirit of piety is envisioned as man's duty. Also, one must not forget that, according to Radhakrishnan, the world is no mere illusion for the pious Hindu.

It might also be argued that the ending of *Siddhartha* is more Taoistic than Indian, and it would be appropriate to quote Lao-tse's saying that the gentlest overcomes the strongest. In the following years Hesse more and more turned to Chinese philosophers, and in *The Bead Game* they replaced the Indians. At the same time he no longer found any contradiction between the Taoistic view of the world and the essense of Christianity. He realized that Lao-tse would have fully understood the *Sermon on the Mount* and could have uttered the promise that "the meek shall inherit the earth."

8 · Existence in the Modern Age

WHENEVER HESSE wanted to describe the meaning of human existence, he chose a locale removed from the contemporary scene, for he felt that this truth could be visualized only at a distance. In *Siddhartha* he clothed it in Indian dress. In *Narcissus and Goldmund* he transposed it into medieval surroundings. In *The Journey to the East* and *The Bead Game* he led his readers to Utopia. The problem itself, however, was neither Indian nor medieval nor Utopian. It was of urgent, contemporary immediacy, and any Romantic expression of it was merely a literary disguise. Between *Siddhartha* and *Narcissus and Goldmund,* Hesse was driven to state his message three additional times in modern form to make it pertinent. These were *Kurgast, The Trip to Nuremberg,* and *Steppenwolf.*

Yet any direct expression of his existential problem also exposed the poet to the danger of losing himself in the subjective and the autobiographical. He did not avoid it successfully in every case. Of the three stories, *Kurgast (In a Health Resort,* 1925) is the least satisfactory. It shows its autobiographical origins most visibly and reads more like a diary and a notebook than an accomplished work of art. The story resulted from a trip in 1923 to the Swiss health resort of Baden, where Hesse hoped to cure his sciatica. Its original title, *Psychologia balnearia or Glosses of a Baden Kurgast* (1924), perhaps indicated its contents more adequately.

To some extent *Kurgast* was influenced by Jean Paul's story *Dr. Katzenberger's Bath Trip,* which also was concerned with the contrast between a sensitive soul and the cold world of modern civilization, brought to light by a trip to a health resort. If anything, Hesse's contrast with his fashionable surroundings was more violent.

This middle-class atmosphere of mediocre band concerts, tedious gambling rooms, and sumptuous dinners accompanied by shallow conversations, was completely uncongenial to him. The souvenir shops with their inane *objets d'art* were annoying. He did not understand the wealthy coffeehouse *habitués* who in the evening listened "with professed delight to a lecture on the noble simplicity of the Japanese way of life" and possessed at home "the legends of Buddhist monks and the teachings of Buddha in beautiful prints and bindings" (IV, 49).

He was particularly revolted by his next-door neighbors, a Dutch couple. The husband appeared to him the epitome of physical health and of good social behavior, and he began to hate him for his outward superiority. The Dutchman was perhaps one of Multatuli's fat businessmen from Indonesia, who became prosperous by their exploitation of the natives, and Hesse saw in him a representative of bourgeois self-sufficiency. The reader cannot help but be reminded of some of Thomas Mann's figures, of Herr Klöterjahn in *Tristan*, or of Mynheer Peeperkorn in *The Magic Mountain*.

In a way, *Kurgast* may even be called a *Magic Mountain* in a minor key. For in both stories the hero's problem is to set modern civilization in its proper perspective. But the difference between Mann and Hesse lies in their methods of solving the problem. In Mann's case the solution is aesthetic and humanistic. Religion played no important part in his world until the *Joseph* cycle. In Hesse's case, the solution is avowedly religious, and humanism plays only a passing role.

When the poet realizes that his hatred of the Dutchman is wrong, he does not fight it with subtle irony, like Mann, but describes it as a basic moral problem. This hatred is "the genuine, naive, stupid hate which an unsuccessful Christian small businessman harbors against the Jews, or a communist against the capitalists" (IV, 62). It could only be overcome by a loving acceptance of the stranger, the different one, the presumable evil. The way toward this acceptance was opened through

Hesse's discovery that he himself was attracted by the rejected bourgeois world. "I had been exactly too moral, too reasonable, too much bourgeois. . . . I must adapt myself to a norm. I wanted to fulfill demands which nobody even made on me, I wanted to be something or act something that I was not at all" (IV, 103). He therefore was not so very different from the hated Dutchman, and here too he had to realize that the world was one. In contrition he returned to those deepest words of mankind which have expressed the unity as well as the multifariousness of creation by ambivalent symbols.

The Chinese Lao-tse has formulated several such sayings, in which both poles of life seem to touch each other for the flash of an eye-lash. Still more nobly and simply and touchingly the same miracle has been achieved in many words of Jesus. I know nothing so moving in the world as the fact that a religion, a philosophy, a psychological system of education formulates for thousands of years the doctrine of good and evil, of right and wrong ever more finely and ever more rigorously, puts up ever higher demands of righteousness and obedience and finally culminates in the magic insight that in the eyes of God ninety-nine righteous people are less deserving than one sinner in the moment of conversion (IV, 114). [For the highest words of mankind] are those few in which this ambivalence is expressed in magic symbols, those few mysterious pronouncements and parables in which the great contrasts of the world are recognized as necessary and at the same time illusory (IV, 114).

Yet the practical religion of the average modern man is a fighting assertion of the self against the surrounding world.

Oh let those simpletons enjoy themselves who are able to love their own egos and to hate their enemies, and those patriots who have never doubted themselves, because they have never believed themselves to be one whit guilty of all the misery and calamity of their country, but have always blamed the Frenchmen or the Russians or the Jews, it does not matter whom, as long as it is somebody else, some so-called "enemy" (IV, 64).

Nine tenths of all the people are happy in proclaiming this barbaric primitive belief which Hesse opposes with the sacred "Idea of unity, the idea that the whole world is a divine unity and that all suffering, all evil originates only when we as individuals no longer feel to be indissoluble parts of this whole, and when the ego is taking himself too seriously" (IV, 63).

The renewed affirmation of Hesse's essential creed forms the ending of *Kurgast*. The book also contains other interesting observations, but as a whole it is an uneven work. Its style is rambling, its structure haphazard. It must be evaluated chiefly as a forerunner of later works of greater import. The prominent part assigned in it to the teachings of Lao-tse and Jesus signifies a departure from the Hindu predilections of *Siddhartha*. However, Hesse was not completely satisfied with the formula arrived at. It began to look too quietistic, too Schopenhauerean, too negative.

The second of Hesse's stories in modern dress, *The Trip to Nuremberg (Die Nürnberger Reise,* 1926), can be called his parallel to Sterne's *Sentimental Journey*. It too began as an autobiographical venture; a trip to Nürnberg to read from his published works. Since all such public exhibitions were distasteful to him, he chose to reach his destinations by detours. The trip became a return journey through the land of his youth and a relaxing vacation.

It began with five exhilarating autumn days at Locarno, and brought an enjoyable meeting with his Zurich friends and their Siamese treasures. It also subjected him to the spell of his Swabian homeland. A dreamy evening at Tuttlingen reminded the author of the first powerful impression he had received as a boy from a Hölderlin poem. Then the old monastery school at Blaubeuren and the wonderful widening of the Neckar River into the so-called "Blue Pot" (*Blautopf*) recalled the story of a fairy, the lovely Lau, who was supposed to have made her home there. Even afterward Hesse could forget himself in the medieval cities of Ulm and Nürnberg and Augsburg, and spend carefree hours in Munich with congenial friends like the poet Joachim Ringelnatz and Thomas Mann.

The escape was not wholly successful. At Baden, in Switzerland, the author's mail caught up with him, bringing requests for magazine articles and flattering letters from young writers inviting him to read their manuscripts. Later, the appointments for the lectures had to be kept. In Blaubeuren he found the subterranean passage of the lovely Lau blocked by cement. The Gothic beauty of ancient Nürnberg was surrounded "by a large, unlovely, desolate business quarter" (IV, 174), where automobiles and motor cycles were making an infernal noise. "I saw everything now enveloped by the exhaust fumes of these dreadful machines, everything undermined, everything vibrating with a life which I can only describe as hellish and inhuman, everything ready to die, ready to become dust, prone to down-fall and destruction" (IV, 175). This in 1927 was a rare prophetic vision. Romantic enchantment had been despoiled, leaving its weaver the need for being brutally outspoken against its ravish-ers. From now on, rather than be entertained, his audiences should be shocked, the disturbing telephones should be torn from the walls, compulsory education which was responsible for this barbaric civilization, should be abolished, and the dese-crated land should be returned to nature.

Yet in this story Hesse found it easier to cope with his black moods (he was disturbed less deeply than in *Kurgast*), and he found a ready answer in humor. "With laughter, with not taking reality seriously, with continuous awareness of its de-structability, this modern life could be tolerated. At some time in the future the machines would be running amock against each other, the arsenals would unload their stuff, and in the same spot where today stands a metropolis, grass would grow again and weasel and marten would slink past" (IV, 166).

The book ends with the emotional release gained by watch-ing the celebrated Munich clown Karl Valentin demonstrate in incomparable fashion the insufficiency of human reason. With ironic detachment the author is able to face modern life once more. "Where will I go now? By how many days will I succeed in delaying my return? I will probably continue my trip for a long time, perhaps through the whole winter, perhaps through my whole life" (IV, 181).

The Trip to Nuremberg is written in a light vein and can be described as a humorous counterpiece to the more serious *Kurgast*. It is also more accomplished in style. The theme of the conflict between romantic recourse to the past and modern existence is repeated again and again, and grows more painful with repetition. But each repetition achieves a measure of mastery of the conflict. The author first attempts to flee from it, then he is willing to face it, then he tries to master it by simple irony. Finally, he dissolves the conflict with real humor, and the painful situation of the moment is subsumed in a general acceptance of life as a journey into the unknown.

The story is far removed from any simple, artless tale of personal experiences. In the beginning it might appear as if the theme is merely one of artistic existence. There are extended discussions of the need of the creative writer to wait for inspiration and to shun all such mechanical disciplines as train schedules and lecture dates. Later we realize that the real theme is much more inclusive: it is the salvation of man's independent spirit from the logistic efficiency of modern civilization; a civilization which he has established in order to make his life easier, but which threatens to engulf him and reduce him to a mere cog in a mechanical system.

This is an old Romantic theme, treated by Jean Paul in *Schmelzle's Trip to Flaez* and by E. T. A. Hoffmann in *Master Flea*. But the form in which Hesse has faced the problem is modern. He not only speaks of railroads and mail schedules, of automobiles and telephones, but even anticipates the destruction of historic cities by aerial bombardment. That he still manages to save himself from the heedless monster, is testimony to the strength of his creative impulse and his faith in a transcendent meaning of life.

The fugue-like structure extends through sentences which may sound redundant to a superficial reader but actually are built on the principle of intensification by increasing outspokenness. In one sentence Hesse fervently implores the Lord not to make him lose his humor: "Let me as your lowest servant do my share that Germany may finally close again its public schools, that Europe may work energetically at the reduction of its birthrates!" (IV, 169). In this ironical sentence the second dependent clause does not merely repeat the first one; it increases its effectiveness by conducting the reader's view from "Germany" to the larger "Europe" and from the regulation of a technical detail to the regulation of the underlying biological factors.

In the next sentence the wish is repeated, this time in a personal vein: "Instead of the money for these lectures, instead of the fame and the flatteries, grant me a mouthful of fresh air for breathing" (IV, 169–170). Here the first "instead" refers to a technical method of appreciation, the second, to the hated appreciation itself. The end of the sentence once more takes up the theme of the first "instead" in its most general, most unconditioned, form: "Grant me a mouthful of fresh air." By a widening and narrowing encirclement of the theme, the fugue has reached full swell.

What has been demonstrated here in a few sentences could be shown on every page. Hesse's art is an art of variation in heightening or in lowering keys. Sometimes his theme is repeated over the whole keyboard. That a master like Thomas Mann has acknowledged the artfulness of this style, should make the reader wary of carping, superficial criticism.

To some extent the happy mood of *The Trip to Nuremberg* can be attributed to the fact that Hesse's personal situation had improved materially since the first Montagnola summers. The revaluation of the mark had led to greater financial security. In 1923 Hesse's three sons were inducted into the Swiss Army, and he himself gave up his German citizenship, which he had retained even after the German surrender. Since he now realized that the new German republic was denounced by most of his fellow countrymen and that the lesson of the war was lost on them, it was easy for him to renounce his German citizenship. When he was elected to the newly founded Prussian Academy of Letters in 1926, Hesse came in as a foreign member. He continued to look at German politics with suspicion and resigned from the Academy four years later. He could not support a republic evolving further and further from democracy.

Hesse was by this time completely at home in Switzerland. He had a few old friends and was also making new ones. In the summer months from 1923 to 1931 he often visited Alice and Fritz Leuthold, the Zurich couple, whom he called his two beloved Siamese. They owned a collection of Asiatic works of art from their long sojourn in Siam which reminded Hesse of his childhood surroundings.

In other months he visited the quiet Bern historian Friedrich Emil Welti, to whom he later dedicated the poem "Organ Play" (V, 760). Among other friends of Hesse were Georg

Reinhart, the Winterthur patron of the arts, the cotton merchant Volkart, Max Wassmer of Bremgarten castle, and the
Zurich patrons Elsy and Hans C. Bodmer.

New friends were found in the writer Hugo Ball and his wife
Emmy Hennings Ball. The former wrote a sympathetic biography of Hesse in 1927 which he presented to his friend on his
fiftieth birthday. During his lifetime Hugo Ball was for the
poet a model of sincere friendship. In spite of their differences
both writers were religiously motivated, and both viewed the
war as a breaking down of the European tradition. Another new
friend was Thomas Stearns Eliot, who was attracted by Hesse's
penetrating analysis of Dostoevski as the prophet of the European catastrophe. Certain verses of *The Waste Land* were
prompted by this analysis (see Eliot's note to lines 367–
377).

All of these friends helped Hesse to overcome his isolation,
but they did not wholly save him from introspection and from
a self-criticism that was severe at times, especially when he
viewed his previous efforts as a writer. When in 1921 Hesse
brought out a new selection of his poems, he rejected most of
his lyric production as halfhearted and unsuccessful. And when
his publisher suggested an edition of Hesse's collected works,
the poet declined. He did not want to republish writings he now
considered ridiculous and worthless; far too self-centered and
arrogant.

Hesse's marital difficulties were not yet solved satisfactorily
either. In 1923 he divorced his first wife, but that did not end
his troubles. Almost immediately he attempted a new marriage,
with Ruth Wenger, daughter of Lisa Wenger, the Swiss writer.
Although he believed that he had known her long enough to as-
sure contentment, he still had to find out that he could not
get along with her either, and the marriage lasted only a few
months. The somber moods could not be excluded. Some of
them he overcame by writing such poems as

Einsamer Abend	Lonely Evening
In der leeren Flasche	In the empty bottle
und im Glas	and in the glass
Wankt der Kerze Schimmer.	The glow of the candle flickers.
Es ist kalt im Zimmer.	This room is cold. The rain

Draussen fällt der Regen weich   Is sifting softly onto
   ins Gras.   the grass.
Wieder legst du nun zu kurzer   Now, to rest a little while,
   Ruh   Chilled and sad you lie down
Frierend dich und traurig   again.
   nieder.   Morning and even come again,
Morgen kommt und Abend   As they always do,
   wieder,   But never you.
Kommen immer wieder,
Aber niemals du.

Such verses can no longer be called Romantic. The folk-song meter and the facile lyricism are gone. The structure of the stanzas has become irregular, and in later poems of this period was given up entirely. Ornate expression has yielded to simplicity. Nature is no longer employed indiscriminately as a metaphor for personal emotions. It has assumed an existence of its own and has become a point of reference rather than a mode of speaking. This separation of man from his surroundings provides the poems of Hesse's second period with a dramatic rather than a lyric quality.

The dramatic effect is especially noticeable in the poems assembled in "Krisis" (V, 688–702). Here a feverish inner disturbance has destroyed the last traces of melody and created passionate free-verse monologues vacillating between uninhibited sensuousness and a fervent desire to overcome it. This disturbance also prevented simplicity of statement and forced the poet to employ a more involved syntax.

Hesse was not able to master all of his dark moods in evenly balanced verses. Again and again they returned to torture him, and he was forced finally to face them without shield or cover in *Steppenwolf*.

9 · Purgatory

SHORTLY AFTER the appearance of *The Trip to Nuremberg,* Hesse's readers were startled by another novel with a theme taken from modern civilization. It was named *Steppenwolf* (Wolf of the Steppes, 1927) and paralleled *Kurgast* both in seriousness and looseness of structure. Yet the sketchiness of *Kurgast* had been journalistic; it had remained a diary which never matured into coherent form. The disjointedness of the new work however was more apparent than real. It presented the appropriate and perfect form for an unfathomable enigma. *Steppenwolf* not only questioned the unimportant personality of Hesse and his calling as an artist, it also questioned man in his modern manifestations and even doubted the value of human existence. The mood of passive acceptance which had produced *Siddhartha* had yielded to a painful re-examination of all life.

The hero of *Steppenwolf* is Harry Haller, whose initials are those of Hermann Hesse. But although three fourths of the book is taken up by Harry Haller's notes written in the first person, the work is preceded by an introduction which sets the episodes in proper perspective.

The first part of the novel is written by the nephew of Harry Haller's landlady. The young man describes Haller objectively, from the point of view of the solid citizen who has found his station in life. To him, Harry Haller was an odd character whose life lacked direction and purpose. He was personally neat, but did not keep his room very tidy and called himself a wolf from

the steppes, a "steppenwolf." His health was precarious, and
he evidently was neurotic and unsociable. One day he left his
lodgings without warning or farewell and never retured.

Harry Haller left some notes in his room, the first part of
which serves to introduce us to his own point of view. He describes his life as the lonely existence of a beast of prey who
has revolted against modern bourgeois culture, although he accepts its comforts and depends on it for subsistence. He sees
it dissolving into a chaotic state, hovering at the brink of an
abyss, and is fully prepared to end his meaningless life by suicide.

On his walks through the city Harry Haller discovers an
advertisement for a "Magic Theatre. Entrance not for Everybody." A sandwich man of the theater hands him a "Tract
about the Steppenwolf." In this astonishing pamphlet Harry's
own predicament is analyzed from the timeless point of view
of the "Immortals" who have achieved the unity of life to
which Harry has aspired in vain.

The modern individual is in a chaotic condition. He belongs in part to the compromising bourgeois world. But he is
also a wild, primitive animal unassimilated to civilization and
heading toward destruction; in a word a "steppenwolf." The
irony of the situation derives from the fact that civilization
would never have reached its high status if there had not always
been "steppenwolf," lonely rebels frustrated by their own im-
perfections and therefore goading themselves to ever better solutions.

This war between two mutually hostile states of mind goes
on without end. Intellect is forever fighting with passion; sharp
reason is clashing with wolfish sensuality; conscious conformity
to the bourgeois world is wrestling with subconscious rejection.
At times, the intellect succeeds in chaining the wolf. Then
again the wolf, tasting blood, tears lose and seeks ravenous
satisfaction in sensuous orgies and destructive wars. Modern
man does not want war, but is nevertheless conducting it.

Haller has ignored the wolf for too long a time. He has
built up an overcharged pressure in his soul, which will finally
erupt destructively. But if he should allow that to happen, his
humanity would be extinguished, and he would sink to the level

of an animal. He must therefore try to overcome his neurosis by humor, by not taking the contradictions of his life too seriously, and by realizing that they are but passing manifestations of a fundamental unity.

Theodore Ziolkowski has shown that this three-part introduction corresponds to the first movement of a sonata and has a sonata form. The introduction composes exposition, development, and recapitulation. Then the sonata continues with a second movement which transposes the theme into rich orchestration. It is concluded by a third movement culminating in a tentative solution, in agreement with the solution recommended in the "Tract."

The structure of the seond movement is contrapuntal. Although it takes place in real life, a symbolic, unrealistic interpretation of this reality is always present. The objective confines of the real world are transfused by Harry Haller's subjective interpretation of it, and his attitudes are limited by the realities of the objective world. But the contradictions tearing his life apart represent no simple dichotomy, as Goethe was wont to describe in his *Faust*. Actually, the modern state of mind oscillates not merely between the two poles, but between numerous sets of poles. Civilization has become a cemetery where Jesus Christ and Socrates, Mozart and Haydn, Dante and Goethe are faded names on rusty tin plates (IV, 264). Modern man no longer orients himself from fixed points of reference.

Hesse presents a pitiless picture of contemporary pluralism, to which his studies of Nietzsche, Dostoevski, and psychoanalysis, and his meditations on Indian philosophy each contributed its share, but which has its final roots in the basic Christian doctrine of man's sinfulness, and might therefore be called Kierkegaardian. (However, Hesse's ideas are far removed from Kierkegaard's religion of fear.) Hesse has absorbed this doctrine in his childhood. As given, the statement is modern and could not have been written without an acquaintance with Hesse's favorite literature, but its contents are ageless and are already contained in the biblical plaint that man is evil from childhood.

The average, traditional Christian drugs himself with the hope that man can overcome his sin by a righteous, moral life led according to the *Ten Commandments*. But already the *Sermon on the Mount* has shown conclusively that an absolutely pure, unselfish life makes superhuman demands, and that the attempt to achieve it borders on absurdity. Hesse adds a modern touch to the basic teachings of Christ by using the arsenal of psychoanalysis. Subconscious emotions cannot long be suppressed without the danger of violent eruptions. World War I was such an eruption. And the rise of Soviet man is another disturbing, though less violent, result of the long suppression practised by European culture.

Harry Haller also finds it necessary to give rein to his suppressed sensuality and face the resulting chaos. Detours and excuses are no longer permitted; the way leads into the midst of the fray. *Steppenwolf* literally signifies a walk through hell— through the inferno of the modern soul—with the will to overcome it. But this modern Dante has no Vergil to guide him. He is introduced into the lower world by the unpoetic Hermine.

On the conscious level, Hermine is a woman of the streets who helps Harry Haller to overcome his inhibitions and leads him into the world of sensuality with its pleasures and temptations. He learns how to dance. He is befriended by the amoral saxophone player Pablo. He sleeps with the prostitute Maria. Pablo even suggests homosexual excesses and introduces him to cocaine and other drugs. This new world of sensuous excesses culminates in a masked ball, which becomes a veritable witches' sabbath. The cellar room of the inn where it takes place is decorated to look like hell, and the members of the jazz band in this hell are dressed as devils.

However, on the subconscious level Hermine represents Harry Haller's double, his "shadow." As Harry is the male counterpart of Hermann, so Hermine is his female counterpart. She personifies Harry's suppressed lower self which at times completely overpowers him. He then loses his identity, a fact symbolically expressed by the description of Hermine as a hermaphroditic being (IV, 299, 315, 317), and even more succinctly by her adoption of boyish dress as a disguise (IV, 359–360). For a time Harry seems to enjoy his steppenwolf existence to the full amid all the inanities of modern jazz civilization.

But then dawn breaks, and a new theme introduces the
third part of the story, the "Magic Theatre." Like the third
movement of a sonata it concentrates on a solution. Harry and
Hermine are left behind by the revelers. Pablo now leads the
couple on. They are intoxicated by wine and champagne, and
also by drugs, so that the borderline between reality and imagination is erased and the two spheres combine and recombine. The
world becomes a magic theater where the unity of the sensuous
and the spiritual is practised. This is symbolized by the fifteen
sideshows of the theater which are comparable to a penny
arcade. Here everything runs together, sexual and homosexual
love, pacifism and ruthless pursuit of war.

Man in the role of an animal trainer puts the steppenwolf
through his paces. Then the steppenwolf takes the dominating
role and lets man crouch and jump. Man as a technical inventor
insults the ear with the cacophony of radio music, but the music
somehow evokes the divine melodies of Handel. The world of
the soul—for this is the Magic Theatre—not only contains all
the libidinous and destructive urges but the creative and unselfish impulses as well. It is not only the world of Pablo and
his prostitute friends, but also the world of Goethe and Mozart.
How can one find purpose and direction here? How is the
chaos to be faced?

In a final effort, Harry tries a one-sided solution. In his
dream world he takes the side of the spirit and stabs Hermine.
This appears to be right, in part, as she certainly does not represent his whole self and is an obstacle to complete integration.
But it is also wrong, since the sensual part of man cannot be
entirely suppressed; man cannot live as a pure spirit either.
Harry the idealist is similarly condemned; we see him standing
in a prison yard before a newly erected guillotine, and the
public prosecutor pronounces his sentence in front of the execution witnesses.

Yet the sentence is not death, but eternal life. Harry is condemned to go on living and to try to find his unified self. He
can find it only by looking through all the disguises of life and
by not taking any one of them seriously, be they completely
sensual or completely spiritual. He must realize unity within

all the multiplicity, and he can do this only in an attitude of humor.

Mozart instructs Harry to learn to live and to laugh (IV, 413). And Pablo, into whom Mozart diffuses at the end of the opium dream, berates him for having destroyed the humor of his little theater and for having been unable to treat Hermine with more detachment (IV, 414). To be sure, Harry Haller has not committed suicide and at times has even managed to laugh about the steppenwolf (IV, 371–372). But he has not sustained this attitude. His first attempt at humor has been unsuccessful, and he will have to start his game again from the beginning; he will have to go through the hell of his soul again. But one day he will be able to play the game better and know how to laugh. "Pablo was waiting for me. Mozart was waiting for me" (IV, 415). Thus *Steppenwolf* does not present a firm solution, but ends with the hope of one, and is therefore a positive step forward.

The meaning of the story will escape a reader accustomed to realistic plots and narratives pursuing a single line of thought. But the modern reader conditioned to Freudian dream analysis and Romantic symbolism will readily understand it. He must, to be sure, be warned against dogmatic interpretations in terms of particular psychological theories. Hermine must not be understood as a mother image.

Although the Oedipus complex played a decisive part in Hesse's early writings, it was no longer important after *Demian* and *Kinderseele*. Hesse's female figures from *Klingsor* on are representations of the sexual side of mature man, and his problem no longer is the conquest of an incestuous love for his mother, but the integration of his mature *libido*. The very name of Hermine characterizes her as a representative of the libidinous *anima*, and her killing signifies an unsuccessful attempt to suppress the *libido*.

For the Hesse of 1927, a complete victory over the chaos appeared more remote than ever. He was well aware that the end of the modern hell had not yet been reached, and he lived in fear of a second world war. He was deeply disturbed by the emergence of a totally disintegrated Soviet type of man and the rise of mechanical conformity among the bourgeoisie. Both were pseudo solutions, poor substitutes for a real integration of the individual into society. They did not lastingly overcome the sin of exclusion.

Only the saints, the "Immortals" of the story, had achieved complete integration, and sainthood in Franciscan or Indian form had definite attractions for Hesse. Yet it had never been granted to him, and it presupposed a degree of selfless renunciation which he was unwilling to give. Only the saint can confess in the hope of overcoming his self and being united with God. Heavenly grace has granted him the strength to mute his will and to become a complete manifestation of the Divine. But the artist, as any ordinary man, can never overcome his self; his confession leads him nowhere. For the artist, confession is almost an end in itself. He needs continuous personal justification and the act of confession gives him enjoyment.

Hesse knew this to be both dangerous and sinful and he continually wrestled with the problem, but he could not overcome it. For better or worse he remained the complete artist. His hell was an artist's hell, and there were times when he could forget that it was a hell and delight in being a fallen angel, a Cain, or a Satan proud of his sin. He could never surrender his ego and atone completely. His fate was the fate of a rebel who protested. Not for nothing was he born a Protestant and raised in a sectarian spirit.

The perfection of an ideal existence would require a perfection of form. But the imperfection of artistic existence precluded any harmony. Hesse therefore deliberately chose a musical form. Such musical structure is not without precedent in narrative literature. Its tradition can be traced back to the model provided by Sterne in the stylistic aberrations of *Tristram Shandy*. From him, Jean Paul copied the technique of distracting footnotes, misleading digressions, and independent appendices. Hesse mentions Jean Paul's aeronaut Gianozzo and his army chaplain Attila Schmelzle in his story (IV, 218). Later, E. T. A. Hoffmann used contrapuntal technique more than once. A scene occurs in his *Night Pieces* (1817) in which Donna Anna, from Mozart's *Don Giovanni*, becomes a real person

visiting the author in his theater box. In a similar manner
Mozart comes to life in *Steppenwolf* at the end of his opera
and visits Harry in his box (IV, 401).

Even more significant are similarities between Hoffmann's
Kater Murr ("Murr the Tomcat," 1820) and Hesse's story.
Kater Murr employed contrapuntal technique as a means of
enabling the poet to express the fundamental discord of his
personality. The autobiography of his learned tomcat gave vent
to the poet's philistine moods and was wedged between pages
torn from the life story of conductor Kreisler, which Murr had
used as blotters and which the printer had supposedly mistaken
for regular copy. In these Kreisler fragments, Hoffmann expressed his artistic sufferings and ambitions, which in no manner
could be harmonized with a rational concept of life.

Hesse was, in part, inspired by Hoffmann. His "Tract
about the Steppenwolf" serves purposes which are similar to
the autobiography of Murr the Tomcat. In the original edition
it was even printed on different paper and set in different type.
Hoffmann's device also was used to indicate the hopeless schism
between man's transcendental aspirations and his rational civilization. The dichotomy here was much greater than in *The Trip
to Nuremberg* and therefore called for an entirely different
structure from that of the spiraling fugue.

One can also discover other evidences of Hesse's literary
predecessors in the story. The scene in which the swarthy saxophone player Pablo leads Harry and Hermine away after the end
of the ball, reminds one vaguely of a similar scene in Keller's
story *Romeo and Julia in the Village*, where an equally dark
violinist leads the doomed lovers through the sleeping landscape.
And the scene where Harry stands before his executioners goes
back to Kafka's *Trial* (1925). But the primary antecedents of
Hesse's story are Romantic.

The consistent use of irony to shock the reader from his
self-complacency and to prevent him from merely amusing
himself by a sweet story is Romantic. Sometimes the irony is
gentle and is achieved by slight exaggerations. Harry Haller is
"living neither in palaces nor in proletarian hovels, but with
consistent stubbornness in these extremely decent, extremely
boring, neatly kept nests of the petite bourgeoisie, which smell

of turpentine and soap, and where one is startled, when one has inadvertently banged the door, or is coming in with dirty shoes" (IV, 210). The parallel of "extremely decent" and "extremely boring" here has the effect of making the whole practice of bourgeois neatness ludicrous.

At another point, the duplicity of Haller's existence is revealed in a more shocking manner. When Harry looks at the projected advertisement of the Magic Theatre, the last line reads "Not for everybody"; when he turns back to read it once more, the line has changed to "Only for madmen" (IV, 215). And in the "Tract about the Steppenwolf," the irony is anything but gentle. "He went on two legs, wore clothes and was a man, but strictly speaking he was just a wolf of the steppes" (IV, 224). "Consciously he despised the bourgeois and prided himself on not being one. Nevertheless in many respects he lived entirely in bourgeois style, he had money in the bank and supported indigent relatives, he dressed decently and inconspicuously, even though without particular care, he tried to live on good terms with the police, the tax collector, and similar powers that were" (IV, 235). Here the almost pedantic enumeration of constituent elements of bourgeois existence achieves the ironic effect.

On the other hand, the musical language that characterized *Siddhartha* is rarely found in *Steppenwolf*. Instead, we often meet with strident disharmonies. When Harry Haller follows a funeral procession, it leads to "a modern patented cement cemetery complete with crematory and all the other gadgets." The parson's clerical gown is called "the black uniform of his profession," and the parson takes pains "to bring the mourning party into the proper mood and to force them to genuflect before the majesty of death" (IV, 259). On his return from the cemetery, Harry meets a professor who walks along under the bare trees of the avenue "with the good-natured, but somewhat comical gait of an idealist, a man who has faith" (IV, 263). Later, in the Magic Theatre Harry Haller reads many advertisements of mental pastimes. One of them asks: "Are you uplifting your spirit? Read the Wisdom of the East." Another recommends "The Decline of the West. At Reduced Prices. Still Unexcelled." A third advertises "Games of Solitaire. The Perfect

Substitute for Every Social Activity" (IV, 385-386). Here modern promotion techniques are applied to cultural pursuits, which thereby makes them of dubious value.

It is readily seen that irony is one of the important stylistic devices employed by Hesse and that he is a master in the use of its various tones. Yet, in spite of these links to his Romantic past, Hesse's story was essentially original. No German writer before him had plumbed the depths of man's soul in similar fashion. To be sure, Goethe in the references to the "Mothers" in the second part of *Faust* had alluded to these depths, but he had as readily covered them up again.

Thomas Mann was undoubtedly right in calling *Steppenwolf* as audacious an experiment as James Joyce's *Ulysses* and André Gide's *Faux-Monnayeurs*. It was the first German novel to include a descent into the cellars of the subconscious in its search for spiritual integration. With Freud it recognized the *libido*, and with Jung it discovered in the subconscious a reservoir of spiritual archetypes and formative ideas.

Because of its theme, *Steppenwolf* is part of the modern literature of disillusionment which started with Kafka, Gottfried Benn, and other writers who appeared immediately before World War I. Between the two world wars came the decisive works of James Joyce, Eugene O'Neill, and John Erskine. For them, after the horrors of the first world war and the brutalities of the Communist revolution, a recourse to nineteenth-century sweetness was impossible.

Then followed the brutalities of the Nazi gas chambers and the anguish of German and Allied war bombings which gave birth to a whole literature of despair, characterized by such names as Norman Mailer and Henry Miller, Jean Anouilh and Sartre, Hermann Kasack and Fritz von Unruh. Only for the emotionally blind was cruelty the privilege of one nation or one class. Intelligent readers, therefore, cannot interpret Hesse's story as the saga of an individual neurosis or a private confession. Nor can they solve man's quandary by traditional medieval asceticism or by a Schopenhauerean denial of the will to live.

In his last novel, *The Bead Game*, Hesse himself proved that he had a solution to offer that was more than tentative.

It had been gestating from *Demian* on, but even in *Steppenwolf* was not yet fully defined. The conclusion of *Klingsor's Last Summer* was ironical. *The Trip to Nuremberg* ended in skeptical amusement. *Steppenwolf* dismissed its readers with a faint ray of humor. Was there perhaps more? The answer could come only from works presenting an overall perspective. From *Narcissus and Goldmund* on, the theme of society and cultural activity therefore replaced that of introspection and personal integration.

10 · The Fulness of Art

WITH *Steppenwolf*, Hesse reached the end of his "confessional" period. The poet realized that an exclusive concern with his own soul would never lead to the desired integration of man and society. Unity could be reached only by his immersion in the full stream of life, and in his last great novels he chose to depict life as a whole. At the same time he was aware that contemporary civilization constituted a very poor parable for the envisioned unity. In each case, therefore, he selected a remote locale. The first story took place in the past, the second moved in the world of fancy, and the third portrayed a distant future. In every case he gained detachment and perspective.

Hesse's first great parable, *Narcissus and Goldmund* (*Narziss und Goldmund*, 1929–1930), was taken from medieval life. The conflict between artistic and scholarly existence, between sinful sensualism and ascetic sainthood had been a personal problem of the author from childhood and had already been employed in a medieval frame in the fragment *Berthold*, which appeared in 1908 (I, 831–883). But this conflict reflected general, no longer personal, tendencies of human life and could be understood only as a part of the immense problem of becoming and declining. A cold-blooded logical solution of the conflict was impossible. A valid artistic image of it came closer to the truth.

The conjunction "and" in the title *Narcissus and Goldmund* indicates the absence of any intention by Hesse to set up a specific example for everyone. Hesse is no dogmatist. To be sure, the vagaries of Goldmund's life are so interesting that in many chapters Narcissus plays a secondary role. Yet Goldmund cannot achieve his individual goal without the help of Narcissus and, of course, Narcissus needs his friend to round out his own life. Each is far from being ideal by himself, and although in the beginning both are disciples of the monastery school of Mariabronn, their essential differences and limitations are apparent and the antagonistic undercurrent in their friendship is very strong.

While Narcissus was dark and haggard, Goldmund was shining and blooming. While Narcissus was an analytic thinker, Goldmund seemed to be a dreamer of a childlike candor. Yet their contrasts were bridged by something they had in common: both were noble souls, both were distinguished before others by visible gifts and marks, and both had been given by fate a special warning (V, 23).

Narcissus is predestined to become a scholar. He is looking everywhere for differences and definitions; he represents the fatherly side of man. Goldmund, on the other hand, is of motherly origin and has to live in the concrete. As Narcissus tells him: "To you belongs the bounty of life, to you the juice of the fruits, to you the garden of love, the beautiful country of art. Your home is the earth, as ours is the idea. You are running the danger of drowning in sensuality, while we could suffocate in airless space. Your are an artist, I am a thinker" (V, 51).

Young Narcissus' abstract and precocious differentiations rouse Goldmund painfully from the warmth of his dreams, but they also help him realize that subconsciously he is seeking the world of his mother and that his aim can never be the priesthood At the end of his novitiate, Narcissus takes final vows and starts his prescribed ascetic exercises. He sees ahead of himself a life of service to the spirit, although he is aware of its one sidedness.

Goldmund, on the other hand, runs away from Mariabronn, just as Hermann Hesse himself ran away from the school of Maulbronn, after which Mariabronn was fashioned. Goldmund's mother too had left her family to live her life to the full. One day, while Goldmund is gathering herbs in the fields, he meets a young gypsy, who surrenders herself to him. In order to be able to return to her, Goldmund leaves the monastery. But the woman in turn deserts Goldmund to return to her

husband. Thus Goldmund's first experience in the world of the
senses teaches him how unstable and fleeting it is.

Nevertheless he must continue his search for worldly
satisfaction. He has an adventure with a peasant woman before
he joins the household of a knight who needs help in writing
his memoirs. The knight has two daughters, Lydia and Julia.
Lydia falls in love with Goldmund and comes into his bed,
but remains chaste. Julia, who has observed her sister's action,
demands also to be taken into Goldmund's bed, unless he wants
to be found out by her father. Lydia, realizing that she and her
sister will no longer be able to resist their lover, confesses everything to her father, who chases Goldmund away.

On the next lap of his journey, Goldmund meets Victor,
a common thief who is scheming to rob him of the goldpiece
which Lydia had secretly sent after him. Goldmund catches
Victor in the act of stealing and stabs him to death. He hides
Victor's corpse and escapes. Now he has experienced the physical violence of the world; a world which he loves so fervently.

As he wanders on, Goldmund discovers a beautiful statue
of St. Mary and is imbued with the desire to meet its creator.
The artist is Master Nicholas who lives in a great city which
reminds one of Basel, or Constance. Nicholas accepts Goldmund
as his disciple, and the youth soon fashions a statue of the
Disciple John, whose features are actually those of Narcissus.
Master Nicholas realizes Goldmund's possibilities and decides
to admit him to the guild and to give the young man his
daughter in marriage. But Goldmund does not want to live a
bourgeois life and deserts his master.

Goldmund does not find greater happiness in his new adventure, but experiences instead the world of the Black Death.
He meets Robert, a vagabonding cleric, and Nell, whom Robert
has saved from a pest-ridden town. For a time the three live
together in a country cottage. When Nell herself contracts the
disease, Robert flees, but Goldmund remains and nurses her
until her death. He then burns the hut together with the
corpse.

Now Goldmund returns to the city of Master Nicholas.
On his journey he meets the Jewess Rebecca. Her father was
burned by the Christians who blamed the Jews for the pesti-

lence. She rejects Goldmund's advances, since she desires only
to die, and he respects her wishes and leaves her alone. In the
city he is informed that Master Nicholas also has fallen victim
to the disease. Then Goldmund catches a glimpse of Agnes, the
governor's mistress. He pursues her until she admits him into
her bedchamber. But on his second visit he is seized by the
watchmen who plan to put him to death the next morning.

A priest comes to give him Extreme Unction, and Goldmund considers killing him and escaping in the priest's habit.
But the priest turns out to be Narcissus, who has become Abbot
John. As Narcissus had promised, he has come to his friend in
the hour of his direst need, when the world of the senses and
the world of violence and disease threaten to engulf him and
steep him in the sin of premeditated murder. Through Narcissus' influence, Goldmund's execution is prevented and he is
freed from jail. Together they return to Mariabronn, where
Goldmund is given a shop in which he can create sculptures.

Once again Narcissus assumes the direction of Goldmund's
destiny and tells him what to do. But he assigns only congenial
tasks and does not condemn Goldmund for his sins. Spiritually,
Narcissus is suffering from the vileness of the world *with* his
friend, but he realizes that the development of Goldmund as
an artist would be impossible without his previous experience
in corpore vili: Art has justified this adventurous and dangerous
life, and Goldmund needs no other forgiveness.

Yet he cannot submit for long to the discipline of monastic
life and he must run away once more into the world of the
senses. Eventually he returns to Mariabronn as a tired old man
whom his young apprentice can scarcely recognize. The world
has become too much for him and he longs for peace, but he
harbors no grudge against fate. He has no faith in a life after
death, but still looks forward to dying: "I am hoping that death
may be real happiness, a happiness as great as the first consummation of love. I cannot get rid of the thought that instead of
death with the scythe it will be my mother who will take me
by my hand and will lead me back into the innocence of non-
existence" (V, 319).

Goldmund dreams that his mother is opening his chest
and loosening his heart. During his whole life he has imagined

that he would ultimately represent her in a creative work of art. Now he realizes that it is she who has created him, and he willingly endures her last ministrations. Will Narcissus ever find home in the same peaceful way, Narcissus who "has no mother?" (V, 322). Goldmund's last words burn in the abbot's breast "like fire" (V, 322).

The end of the novel expresses the same belief in love as the ultimate reality as does the last verse of Dante's *Divine Comedy* or those lines of Goethe's *West-Eastern Divan* where the poet is anticipating his dissolution and extinction "in contemplation of the love eternal." Only a motherly image was able to convey such a sentiment, and Hesse chose it with an unerring artistic instinct. At the same time his choice could be defended in the light of Jung's theories which always emphasized the female aspects of man's image of the divinity.

Yet it is clear that Hesse's turn to a motherly divinity in this novel no longer bears the earmarks of an unsolved Oedipus complex; of a violent rebellion against the world of the father. The early stories had sought release from fatherly strictness in the arms of motherly nature, and *Demian* had ended in a symbolical union with the divine mother. The fatherly world, the world of the spirit, at that time was seen as ending in "convulsions and suffering and war" (cf. the poem "Return," V, 644).

Hesse has now come to accept the fatherly spirit as being necessary also. To be sure, Narcissus, whose very name seems to indicate an egocentric preoccupation with the mysteries of his individuality, realized his lack of creativity and his lack of love. "My life has been poor in love, I have lacked the best. . . . I am not unjust against men, I am taking pains to be fair and to be tolerant towards them, but I have never loved them" (V, 316). Still, without Narcissus' roving participation there would have been no direction or purpose to Goldmund's life.* For just as Goethe knew that the path to the creative "Mothers" was also the path into the chaos which gave birth to everything, Hesse was aware that the artist was always in danger of losing himself in chaos.

On his journey through life's unplumbed mysteries, Gold-

---

* The name "Goldmund" is the German equivalent of the Greek "Crysostomos," the name of Goldmund's patron saint.

mund is forever skirting the abyss and wooing temptation and sin. He needs Narcissus to give him tasks and measure so that he can understand his needs and appreciate his abilities. Goldmund confesses in the end that he has always loved Narcissus and that he has been searching for him through half of his life (V, 317).

It is hard to say which one of the two stands in greater need of the other, although the pointer of the scales perhaps balances slightly toward Goldmund, who symbolizes Hesse's personal artistic approach to life. This "perhaps" is the poet's final word in the conflict between the fatherly and the motherly principles of life. Ultimately, life is a continuous oscillation between Yin and Yang, as a Far Eastern sage might express it, or between systole and diastole, as Goethe would have said. The approach of the occidental to the oriental world appears to be complete.

Yet there is no oriental stress on withdrawal from the world and on ascetic concentration upon the mystic union. Hesse has become neither a Buddhist nor a hermit. He is Eastern only insofar as the *Bhagavad-Gita* is also Eastern. The stress is still on active mastery of the world, even though this means suffering and sin and error. There is still the conviction that man has to do the work of God and has to embrace all the world with his love.

Goldmund's love is not the love of an ascetic. It is avowedly sensual and sexual. But he knows that sensual love "can become the vessel of the soul" (V, 318) and does not pursue it as an end in itself. Hesse's concern is far removed from the current preoccupation with sex to the exclusion of everything else. He has clearly broken with orthodox Christianity, and his religion can be called Christian only when one defines Christianity as a wholly undogmatic religion of love (cf. also VII, 373). Absent is the belief in the myth of Christ's life and the divinity of Jesus, in the redemption of sins through his death on the cross, and in resurrection and personal immortality. (Goldmund is not saved by Christ's redemption.)

Still, Hesse has by no means renounced the Christian spirit. He has not turned into a pagan who worships God through orgies. With him, the path of erotic art toward the inscrutable divinity is, to be sure, one way, but it is not the only way. To the same degree, ascetic dedication to the pure spirit is not the only way, although it is right for some people. For Hesse mysticism has never been an esoteric attitude confined to a few "spiritual" men. On the contrary, his "natural" men are just as fervent seekers for God as are his "spiritual" men. Both Narcissus and Goldmund have the same destination, but they reach it in different ways.

As Narcissus states at the end: "We philosophers try to approach God by divesting Him of the world. You however approach Him by loving His creation and producing it again. Both ways are human ways and therefore unsatisfactory, but the way of art is the more innocent one" (V, 300). "We two, dear friend, are sun and moon, are sea and land. Our aim is not to combine, but to realize each other and to learn to see and honor in the other what he is: one's own contrast and complement" (V, 49).

Because the theme of the novel is the development of two human beings, its narrative structure is determined by the stages of human development. But, since the two lives are inextricably interwoven, this structure is anything but simple. Narcissus is portrayed from the beginning in an advanced state of development. He has accepted the world for what it is and is consciously filling his place in it. Yet we know that in spite of his relative maturity he has by no means reached the ultimate stage of sainthood. Even in the end Narcissus has not achieved perfection; he is still on the way to it. The outward stages of his life are clearly marked, but they are of minor interest and are therefore mentioned only in passing.

In the main, Narcissus' life serves as a frame for the life of Goldmund. It is elaborated in the beginning as well as the end of the story. In between, the life of Goldmund is developed in stages, similar to those of Siddhartha. To be sure, Goldmund's innocence is not Siddhartha's childhood innocence among gentle Brahmins. It is the innocence of nature which follows its sensual impulses without restraint. One has to be free from traditional preconceptions to realize that Goldmund's first sexual experiences with the gypsy Lise are basically innocent. A different note enters only with the daughters of the knight, where the conflict between the spirit and the flesh, between what is traditionally "good" and traditionally "evil," plays a decisive role.

The murder of Victor, although committed in self-defense, clearly marks the fall from grace. Then follows the conscious dedication to accepted evaluations of life and work under the guidance of Master Nicholas. There is just as conscious abandonment during the period of the Black Death and the episode with the governor's courtesan. Acquiescence to God's will is begun by Goldmund's return to Mariabronn, but it is not achieved without major struggles. The vision of reintegration and a regained "innocence" comes to Goldmund only in his dying hours.

One realizes that Hesse's original scheme of human development is still visible, but one also finds that it cannot be applied without bold simplifications. Ultimately Goldmund's life defies simple logic. The fabric of his soul is too rich to be dominated by a single strain. There are knots in its skein and minor weaving faults in the form of unsolved riddles and interrupted developments. To be sure, the structure is fugue-like, as the basic theme of Goldmund's relation to sensual reality is repeated in different keys, until the final repetition leads to an integration of the dissonances and their dissolution in a new harmony. But the theme of the fugue is complicated, and the ensuing variations are richly ornamented. While *Siddhartha* is characterized by an almost Gothic simplicity, *Narcissus and Goldmund* could be described as baroque. But one has to describe it as a calm and balanced baroque.

The novel is richer in colorful descriptions than most of its forerunners. *Siddhartha*, for example, clothes the real world in a haze of unreality. *Narcissus and Goldmund* brings the world of the late Middle Ages vividly alive. It is the fifteenth-century world of Nicholas of Cusa, when unorthodox interpretations of Christianity were tolerable, although few people in that day found fault with pogroms. Hesse's picture of the Middle Ages is certainly not nostalgic. Christian cruelties against the Jews are not excused, but condemned (IV, 230–231; 274–275), and the ravages of the Black Death form an important part of the general background. However, the fascinating and elevating aspects of the Middle Ages are equally emphasized. The touching innocence of medieval men and women, the simple piety of medieval art, the unspoiled character of the medieval landscape, are present in ever changing images.

Narcissus and Goldmund is replete with fine descriptions of the heath and the forest, of the sun's rising and setting. The image of a village with all its shades of color and sound and odor is evoked in a few pertinent sentences:

Already in the evening of this day he was in a beautiful village, which lay between the river and the red, sloping vineyards by the great highroad. At the gabled houses the pretty framework of beams was painted red, there were vaulted gateways for wagons and alley ways of stone stairs. A smithy threw a red, fiery glow upon the street and broadcast the bright pealing of its anvil. The curious visitor roamed around in all the sideways and byways, he sniffed at cellar doors the scent of the wine barrels and at the river edge the cool, fishy odor of the water, he observed the house of God and the cemetery and did not omit to look around for a useful barn where one perhaps could alight for the night. But first he wanted to try his luck in the parsonage with a request for sustenance (V, 150).

The picture of a fish market is sketched in a few masterly strokes and at once achieved a new, transcendental dimension:

The next day Goldmund could not make the decision to go into the studio. Like on other adverse days he gadded about in the town. He saw the women and the maid-servants go to the market, he particularly loitered at the well on the fish market and watched the fishmongers and their buxom wives, as they were offering their wares for sale and praising its virtues, as they tore the cool, silvery fishes from their tubs and displayed them, as the fishes with mouths gaping from pain and with golden eyes livid with fear calmly became resigned to death or were fighting it in fury and desperation. Like often before he was seized by pity for these creatures and by a sad annoyance at people; why . . . did they not see these mouths, these eyes afraid unto death, these tails wildly slashing about, why not this gruesome, useless struggle of despair, why not this unbearable transformation of the mysterious, wondrously beautiful creatures, as the last, subtle tremor was rippling over their dying skins and they then lay dead and extinguished, spread out as pitiful chunks of meat for the table of the cheerful glutton? (V, 183).

In all of these repetitions there is, however, no redundancy. On the contrary, each new element of the sentence adds a nuance of perception and illuminates or widens the picture. Hesse is likewise a master of the art of visualizing places and personalities with a few, effective adjectives. There is "the haughty, cool maiden Elisabeth" (V, 186). There is gentle Nell, "a sweet playmate, shy and inexperienced, but full of love" (V, 215). There is, in the beginning of the story, the gypsy Lise, the ripe "young woman in a faded blue skirt, with a red kerchief tied around her black hair, with a brown face tanned by the summer" (V, 79). There is little Marie, "a child of fifteen years, a quiet, sickly creature with beautiful eyes, but with a hip injury which made her limp." She receives Goldmund's kiss "reverently, with closed eyes" (V, 199). There is the courtesan Agnes, "his beautiful, royal sweetheart, who looked so haughty and yet could forget herself and abandon herself so much in love" (V, 256).

Never before had Hesse attempted such full pictures of sensual union and completion. Since it is physical as well as spiritual completion, it could be described without vulgar details. Instead of the probing of adolescent curiosity we have here the joyous awareness of maturity. There remains no trace of the nervous frustrations evident in *Peter Camenzind*, in *Gertrude*, in *Rosshalde*, and even in *Demian*.

The novel is so rich in color that it can indulge in long, philosophical passages without fear of dimming its brilliance. A certain didacticism is perhaps inseparable from a novel of development. But in this case it is not obtrusive and does not jar the reader. Because of all the vivid images he experiences in the novel's pages, he accepts the philosophical remarks as a natural evidence of life's fulness. Through this combination of impressive, colorful imagery and lofty philosophy, Hesse's story is a worthy addition to the lengthy series of German novels of growing up (*Bildungsromane*), a reassertion of the problems discussed in Goethe's *Wilhelm Meister* and Keller's *Green Henry*.

The German public was immediately aware of it and read the story with deilght, though perhaps not always with understanding. To be sure, Hesse's style was too descriptive and not creative enough for the average English or American reader, and the story was also too philosophical. The American success of *Narcissus and Goldmund* did not match that of *Steppenwolf* or *Siddhartha*. Perhaps a part of the blame rests with the translator, who chose the meaningless and misleading title *Death and the Lover* for the English rendering of Hesse's novel.

In the summer of 1927 Hesse was fifty years old. His birthday reminded the poet of physical decline rather than spiritual achievement, and he asked that no special note be taken of it. He celebrated the day quietly with a few Swiss friends. Among them was the Austrian art historian Ninon Dolbin, née Ausländer, who was more than twenty years his junior. The poet had corresponded with her since 1926 when they had met by accident. From 1927 they lived together, and in 1931 Hesse married her. This time the marriage lasted. Until his death Ninon remained the intelligent and understanding comrade whom he needed in his sometimes difficult moods. Without her gentle influence the tenor of Hesse's last three novels would scarcely have been so optimistic.

A certain calmness set in, and the Casa Camuzzi no longer suited the mood of Hesse's later years. It had seen too many hours of loneliness and depression. It was also too small and far from comfortable. On a spring evening in 1930, as the poet discussed his housing problems with some friends in "The Ark," Dr. Hans C. Bodmer's house in Zurich, his host laughed at him and said: "That house you surely will get!" (IV, 633). And he ordered a house built in Montagnola according to Hesse's specifications which he leased to the poet for life.

This Casa Hesse was carmine colored, and was therefore called "Casa Rossa." It was situated above Montagnola, apart from the village and hidden behind bushes and trees. Access was possible only by a little-known path. It allowed a wide view of Lake Lugano to its Italian shores, of majestic Monte San Salvatore and Monte Generoso.

Hesse by this time had become famous, and like all modern idols had to take precautions to safeguard his privacy. Although he was not asocial, he did not want curious teen-agers and autograph seekers to intrude upon his personal life. He therefore sought to turn them away at the gate of his hermitage with a notice which read: "Visitors not Welcome." On the house door itself Hesse pasted a longer quotation from Mêng-tzŭ which asked the intruder to pass on as if Nobody lived there. All these measures did not, of course, prevent the insistent from writing letters, and the mere sorting of mail became an unwelcome daily burden. It sometimes took hours to separate important letters from the great pile of missives, many of which could not be answered. It constituted something of a miracle that Hesse's creative life continued at all.

11 · Pilgrim's Progress

LIKE *Narcissus and Goldmund, The Journey to the East* (Die Morgenlandfahrt, 1931) might be desribed as a romantic venture. But again Hesse was by no means trying to escape from modern problems. He simply sought distance and perspective.

The Journey to the East takes place after the end of World War I and bears little resemblance to any travel book. It does not report any real trip to the Orient as did the contemporary travel books by Alfons Paquet, Max Dauthendey, and Hanns Heinz Ewers. The opening paragraphs of the story also set it apart from Count Keyserling's less factual *Travel Diary of a Philosopher* (1919) or from Ferdynand Ossendowski's somewhat fanciful travel accounts. For indeed the East toward which the poet is traveling is a metaphor for the higher, transcendental self.

Hesse introduces himself as "H. H.," who must, of course, be as little identified with the real author as "K." in *The Castle* with Kafka. Both "H. H." and "K." relate their experiences in diary form. H. H. wants to report the history of an expedition in his diary. He describes himself as a participant in a unique journey undertaken by a mysterious League. This League has renounced all "the common-place aids of modern travel such as railways, steamers, telegraph, automobiles, airplanes, etc." (VI, 10), those "modern contrivances which spring into existence in a world deluded by money, number and time, and which drain life of its content" (VI, 15).

The group does not measure its progress by watches. It

does not really need any contrivances, since the aim of its
journey is the fairy-tale world of an imaginary East, "the Home
of Light." Throughout the centuries this procession of believers
and disciples "had been on the way towards light and wonder,
and each member, each group, indeed our whole host and its
great pilgrimage, was only a wave in the eternal stream of human beings, of the eternal strivings of the human spirit towards
the East, towards Home" (VI, 15).

Yet, in spite of these high intentions, the narrator does not
seem to be fully prepared to describe his journey. He possesses
no notes or documents from the time when he made the journey, and he has to admit that even his memories of this period
have faded. Still he takes up his task resolutely, since he believes
in a dedication to the paradoxical. He can approach it only in
a roundabout way.

H. H. does not offer us a straight narrative, but refers
vaguely to "certain episodes of our Journey to the East" undertaken in "a singular attitude of unreality, of readiness for the
transcendental" (VI, 10). He selects a few highlights of the
trip at random, like the "Journey across the Moon Ocean to
Famagusta under the leadership of Albertus Magnus, or perhaps the discovery of Butterfly Island twelve leagues beyond
Zipangu, or the inspiring League ceremony at Rüdiger's grave."
Not one of these reminiscences moves into clear focus. They
remain colorless and are summarily classified as "deeds and experiences allotted once only to people of our time and our zone"
(VI, 11).

The uncertainty is increased by continuous lapses from
imagination into reality, and by repeated efforts to make the
world of fancy more vivid by the introduction of well-known
historical personalities. But the fanciful as well as the real remain blurred, and the narrator does not succeed in a unified
presentation: "I see that the tale cannot be told in this way"
(VI, 34). "There is nowhere a unity, a center, a hub around
which the wheel is revolving . . . everything is only a mass of
separate fragmentary images which have been reflected in
something, and this something is myself, and this self, this
mirror, whenever I have gazed into it, has proved to be nothing
but the uppermost surface of a glass pane" (VI, 35).

Only two episodes of the narrative become clear, one of which belongs to reality. One time a League member expresses doubts and is therefore read out of the company. The narrator treats his case with appreciable sympathy and thereby proves that he too is an unbeliever who merely tries to rise to the state of grace, but has not yet attained it. Reality and super-reality have clearly fallen apart.

The second episode beolngs to the realm of fancy. The League gathers for a celebration at Bremgarten Castle, where its members hear Othmar play Mozart on the grand piano in the great hall, listen to the fairy Armida sing at the fountain, and meet Heinrich von Ofterdingen of medieval romantic fame. Here the reality of the Swiss castle and the assembled contemporaries blends beautifully with the timeless atmosphere of the fairy world. Stylistic mastery of the episode is achieved without efforts:

> The lilac sent its fragrance into my bedroom in the deep of Bremgarten. I heard the river rustle beyond the trees. I climbed out of the window in the depth of night, intoxicated with happiness and yearning, stole past the knight on guard and the sleeping revelers down to the river bank, to the rustling waters, to the white, gleaming mermaids. They took me down with them into the cool, moonlit crystal world of their home, where they played their unredeemed dreams with the crowns and golden chains of their treasure chambers. It seemed to me that I spent months in the sparkling depths, and when I emerged and swam ashore, thoroughly chilled, Pablo's reed-pipe was still to be heard from the garden far away, and the moon was still high in the sky (VI, 26).

However, this beautiful fusion of reality and fancy is not long sustained. Its harmony is destroyed on the unhappy day when Leo, a voluntary servant, defects from the League. Leo helped to carry the luggage and was often assigned to the personal service of the Speaker. All animals were attached to him, and he desired to obtain "Solomon's key which would enable him to understand the language of the birds" (VI, 22–23).

In the dangerous gorge of Morbo Inferiore, Leo is missed, and the value and meaning of everything is threatened: "our comradeship, our faith, our vow, our Journey to the East, our whole life" (VI, 30). The group has also lost an indispensable part of its luggage, and the really important things all appear to have been in the missing bag, which was being carried by Leo. Most importantly, the fundamental and indispensable League charter now appears to be gone. No one knows exactly where the original was, or how it looked, but there existed four or five translations of it made during the founding master's lifetime. The heated disputes about the document are something new and unheard-of in the hitherto perfectly harmonious League. It threatens to dissolve into separate fragments, and the narrator himself is completely frustrated. The first part of the narrative thus ends in violent disharmony.

Again the story might be compared to a sonata, the first movement of which presents two distinct themes in contrapuntal juxtaposition, brought into harmony by the two subsequent movements. The second movement comprises the third and fourth chapters and might be called an andante sostenuto. In it, we return to concrete reality. The narrator attempts to approach his aim "in a practical and reasonable manner" (VI, 37).

He takes his problem to a newspaper friend named Lukas, who in his skepticism calls the League, somewhat disrespectfully, "the Children's Crusade." But he is a well-meaning skeptic and understands fully why H. H. must write the League's history. Lukas himself must write in order to divest himself of his war experience, since he cannot exist without mastering it, and H. H. must write about the League, because it likewise represents to him an essential part of his experience. Its disclosure is an existential task, with the existence of the narrator becoming the real theme of the story. That it is now approached on the plane of reality is a step forward, for it is a step toward humility fully in accord with Leo's observation: "Whoever wants to live long, must serve. He who wants to rule, does not live long" (VI, 28).

In the beginning the narrator wanted to achieve the ultimate by trying to describe the indescribable. He now is more moderate, no longer despising the small and apparently insignificant things. First, he looks up Leo's address in the directory, and finds an Andreas Leo, 68a Seilergraben. Leo actually lives at a real address and has a real occupation as a chiropodist, herb expert, and dog trainer. With this knowledge, the haziness of the first part of the story is replaced by a cogent style of visualization.

At the same time, this very real Leo is connected with the transcendental. When the narrator succeeds in finding him at home, Leo is whistling a tune. "The music was banal, but the whistling was wonderfully sweet, with soft and pleasing notes, unusually pure, as happy and as natural as the songs of birds" (VI, 44). And when Leo walks down the lane, his step is realistically described as "light, effortless, and youthful," but also "in keeping with the evening; it was of the same quality as the twilight" (VI, 45). In other words, Leo is at once a part of his surroundings and a private individual. The secret of his harmonious fusion with his atmosphere is suggested by the lightness and effortlessness of his step. Life, when it is beautiful and happy, is "a game" (VI, 49).

It is not only Leo who plays life as a game, without hurry and without plan. The narrator too has learned to forget himself to some extent and has begun to pay attention to the objective realities. His style has shifted from abstractions and generalizations and a preponderance of attributive adjectives and is concentrating on basic nouns and characteristic verbs. Leo "saunters slowly under the lilacs and acacias" (VI, 46). He sits down on an empty bench and takes from his coat pocket a small round box of white metal, from which he picks a few prunes and dried apricots, which he eats with great savor. Everything in this description is clearly observed, no detail is slighted.

Yet H. H. is far removed from a complete identification with Leo's attitude. Still pursuing his first aim, he excitedly contradicts Leo's assertion that life is a game (VI, 48). He implores Leo to remember their common experiences in the League. When Leo's Alsatian dog Necker appears, the narrator's lack of contact with nature becomes apparent in the dog's complete rejection of him. H. H. is "sick or intoxicated" (VI, 49), while Leo is calm and serene. Since the latter is in complete harmony with unconscious nature, the dog greets him as a friend and equal.

Leo is at a loss what to do with the nervous H. H. and simply walks away, impelled to leave him to his selfish reflections. But already the necessity of completing his history has moved to second place in the narrator's plans. He now hopes to use it as a stepping-stone to his purification and redemption, and thus find the path on which Leo has walked without interruption (VI, 50).

H. H.'s return to the League is told in Chapter Five, the third movement of the story, which resumes the theme of the first part at a higher level. Thus the structure of the novel becomes a spiral comparable to the arrangement of Eichendorff's *Good-for-Nothing* or of Novalis' fairy tale of *Hyacinth and Rosebud*.

To be sure, the ethical and aesthetic perfection of Leo has already become apparent in the natural surroundings of the story's second part. But for the narrator, its complete realization is still distant and can be reached only in the imagination, although in the last analysis the imagined aim must become the guiding light of his real life also. We are again transposed into the world of fancy. This time, however, it is not approached by haphazard, fragmentary recollections, but by continuous, uninterrupted narration.

H. H. is summoned before the High Throne. As his guide, Leo conducts him to a large suburban building with many chambers and passages. They find a gigantic archive in its garret, the walls of which are covered with cupboards containing books and bundles of documents. When Leo sings one of the League songs, the archive and library officials make way for other officials who now proceed to occupy rows of benches gradually ascending toward a High Throne, not yet occupied. Among them the narrator discerns the figures of Albertus Magnus, the ferryman Vasudeva, the artist Klingsor, and others. The narrator stands alone before the High Throne and is immediately addressed by the Speaker.

In the story, every part of this description is concrete and can be fully visualized, yet we are moving in a different dimension. The images change continuously; the visualized details become transcendent and fuse into each other.

The Speaker turns out to be Leo, whose image emanates currents which enter into H. H., while H. H. is on his way "to yield more and more to Leo, to nourish him and to strengthen him" (VI, 76). The essence of this higher dimension is not confining reality, but sacrificing and self-abandoning love. Gradually the narrator enters into its spirit.

While he and Leo were approaching the League building he was still impatient with Leo's detours and roundabout ways. But in the hall of the archives he realizes the utter foolishness of his intention to write a history of the League. Finally, he confesses before the High Tribunal to his lack of humility and stands ready to be condemned.

Of the three judgments offered to him, he selects the hardest, which commands him to consult the archives about himself. He discovers in a niche behind a thin veil dual figures joined by a common back. He illuminates the niche and sees that one half of the statue represents a blurred likeness of himself that could be called "Transitoriness" or "Decay." The other half is strong in color and resembles Leo, the servant and president. The two figures begin to melt into each other, and the substance of his own image in time merely strengthens the image of Leo. "He must grow, I must disappear" (VI, 76). His task is to become ever more loving, ever more understanding of others, ever less self-conscious and egocentric. Now finally the narrator can find peace. Overcome by an infinite weariness he seeks a place where he can sleep.

Yet the general aim of loving, harmonious existence can still be realized in different ways. H. H. does not give up his intention of writing a history of the League, but merely proposes to start it again from more humble beginnings. He will also recover his violin which he sold in his despair. In other words, he remains a poet and writer, although he now has learned to approach his art in an entirely different disposition. He is no longer dedicated to art for art's sake and no longer seeks self-satisfaction in it. It is made clear by H. H.'s designation as an *Anima Pia* that his artistic task is simply a personal expression of a general human goal; namely, the realization of the divine transcendency. Hesse as an artist will remain a pilgrim, and the aim of his pilgrimage is not art, but the "East," east in this case being a metphor for the *unio mystica*.

The unity of ordinary reality and higher transcendency is already indicated by the use Hesse has made of personal ex-

periences. As a rule they are impersonalized by lightly disguised or Latinized names. Morbio Inferiore refers to an illness
(Lat. *morbus*) which has its roots in the subconscious (*inferior*)
regions of the mind and is therefore particularly dangerous,
although it should not present an obstacle to higher aspirations.

Othmar who plays the piano at Bremgarten is the musician
Othmar Schoeck. In other persons taking part in the League
celebration one can recognize Dr. Lang, Hans Albrecht Moser,
Louis Moilliet, and of course Max Wassmer, the lord of the
manor, and his wife Tilly. There are also allusions to Hans C.
Bodmer's house, "Noah's Ark," to the "black king" Georg
Reinhart, the Winterthur industrialist, and to the "two Siamese," Fritz Leuthold and his wife. A clear understanding of
most of these allusions is unessential for the reader, so long
as he receives the impression that H. H. is not moving in thin
air, but through a disguised or translucent reality. More essential is an understanding of the character of Leo. Leo, is, as R.
H. Farquharson has made abundantly clear, Hesse's cat *Löwe*,
although Hesse has borrowed some of the religious authority of
Pope Leo III for the animal.

This favorite cat, who was also portrayed in the epic
Hours in My Garden (V, 340–341), fascinated Hesse by his
typically feline grace and alertness. And, like *Löwe*, Leo is independent and unpredictable. He is not interested in men,
but knows dogs, birds, and also cats very well. Leo here represents H. H.'s second, nonempirical self, his share in the impersonal and transcendental. Leo is closer to God than H. H.'s
empirical self; he is content to sacrifice himself and to serve.
While the empirical H. H. takes himself too seriously, Leo does
not need any philosophical directions represented by a League
charter, and knows instinctively what is right. He can serve
without feeling inferior and has achieved the lighthearted view
of life which neither *Kurgast* Hesse nor Friedrich Klein nor
Harry Haller were able to attain. Life here is conceived essentially as a game (VI, 49), and one is reminded of Friedrich
Schiller's classical assertion that man fulfills his destiny only
when at play (cf. *Letters on the Aesthetic Education of Man*,
1795, letter 15).

It should also be pointed out that in the figure of Leo,

Hesse has found a solution for the problem of the individual's place in the community. For while Leo is independent enough, he is not irresponsible. He is a servant of the higher powers represented by the League. The League to a certain extent has here replaced the Church; it is at once a secularized and spiritualized form of the pietistic *ecclesiola*. Hesse had an ingrained pietistic aversion to organized religion, but he recognized other people's need for it, and in the image of the League he came as close to a religious community as he could. It is characteristic of Hesse that in this community, too, one joins by an "awakening" which is given by "grace." H. H. has access to it as an *Anima Pia*.

Few of the metaphors employed in the story are entirely new. The comparison of life to a journey is an ancient image which gave Bunyan the inspiration for *Pilgrim's Progress* with its detailed descriptions of a Christian traveler's adventures. But Bunyan's book has not contributed any details to the story and probably remained unknown to Hesse. He was, however, familiar with Gotthold Ephraim Lessing's *Nathan the Wise*, which contains the parable of the lost ring which each religion claims for its own. (One is vaguely reminded of this parable by the dispute about the lost League charter.)

More decisively, Hesse was inspired by Novalis' fragmentary novel *Heinrich von Ofterdingen*. Here the hero sets out on a journey in his quest for the blue flower, the symbol of Romantic poetry. In fact, the motto of *Heinrich von Ofterdingen* is quoted in the beginning of Hesse's *Journey to the East:* "Where are we really going? Always home!" (VI, 15). By this motto Novalis wants to indicate that the root of poetry lies in the poet's own breast. His journey leads Heinrich von Ofterdingen into his own past and into the subconscious land of dreams and archetypal reminiscences.

Of course, Jung's psychoanalysis did not exist at the time of German Romanticism, although its founders were deeply interested in what they called the night side of life, and Novalis himself wrote *Hymns to the Night*. In the fairy tale concluding the first part of *Heinrich von Ofterdingen*, Novalis presages the end of Rationalism by an image in which paternal wisdom and female openness to the transcendental are combined. One is also reminded of Kafka's *Castle,* which Max Brod published posthumously in 1926, and with which Hesse had already became intimately acquainted in 1928 (cf. also *Kafka-Deutungen,* [*Kafka Interpretations*], 1956; VII, 469–471).

While Kafka designates himself as "K.," Hesse has described himself as "H. H.," and H. H., like K. in *The Castle,* falls asleep in the end of the novel. But one should not lose sight of the fact that Hesse had used this image as early as 1913 (*Augustus,* III, 285), thirteen years before the publication of *The Castle.* We are also reminded of Kafka by the hierarchy of officials guarding H. H.'s secret. Previously, in Mozart's *Magic Flute* (text by Emanuel Schikaneder), a full freemasonry of high priests had watched Pamino's progress toward self-realization. Hesse was very partial to Mozart, whom he mentioned several times in his story.

The structure of *The Journey to the East* is indebted to another author of the Goethe period, Jean Paul, again one well-known to Hesse and often mentioned by him. In his *Hesperus,* which was a favorite book of Hesse (cf. IV, 815), Jean Paul sets out to write a story, without as yet knowing how it will end. He has to wait for the individual chapters to arrive in a flask hanging at the neck of a dog. This is the so-called "dog mail." The subtitle of the story is accordingly *Hundposttage,* or "dog mail days." The writing of the story in Jean Paul's novel serves as a subsidiary theme indicating the unpredictable character of life.

In Hesse's *Journey to the East* the writing of the story of the League has become the main theme, or at least one of the main themes. Aside from this there are, however, no specific instances of Hesse's borrowing from Jean Paul. And certainly E. T. A. Hoffmann's use of Murr the Tomcat as an embodiment of philistinism was very different from Hesse's use of Leo-*Löwe* as a representation of spiritual wisdom.

Whenever Hesse alludes to his predecessors, he refers to them in general terms. There are numerous such allusions incorporated in *The Journey to the East.* Among other literary figures, Cervantes' Don Quixote is mentioned, Hoffmann's Archivarius Lindhorst, Novalis' Klingsor, Tieck's Almansor, Wolfram von Eschenbach's Parzival, Sterne's Tristram Shandy,

Achim von Arnim's Guardians of the Crown, and Wieland's
Hüon from *Oberon*. Finally, figures from Hesse's own writings
appear again and again, e.g., Hermann Lauscher, Pablo from
Steppenwolf, and Louis the Cruel from *Klingsor's Last Summer*.
This is a well-known device used by Romantic writers everywhere. Even contemporaries like Paul Klee enter the knight-
errantry of the League, and the snake Kundalinda (taken from
Indian legends) may remind one of the snake-god Mukalinda
in Gerhart Hauptmann's *Isle de Notre Dame* (1924). All of
these allusions serve to lend color to the story and to make
the narrator's quest appear less personal and more representative.

They are needed also to achieve distance from the worka-
day world and to make the style transparent. Hesse's sentences
are generally simple. He avoids the involutions of Thomas
Mann's style and prefers paratactical clauses, appositions, and
enumerations. But the end effect is the achievement of trans-
parency. The clarity of the vision gains depth and becomes
mysterious.

> During the times I remained alone, I often found again places
> and people from my own past. I wandered with my former betrothed
> by the wooded shores of the Upper Rhine, I caroused with the
> friends of my youth in Tübingen, in Basel, or in Florence. Or I
> was a boy and went with my schoolmates to catch butterflies or
> to watch an otter. Or my company consisted of the favorite figures
> of my books. Almansor and Parzival, Witiko or Goldmund, or
> Sancho Pansa rode by my side. Or we were guests of the Bar-
> mekides (VI, 23).

The individual clauses of this passage are all clear and
understandable, but their combination makes reality disappear
and transposes us into a world of memory. Then the next sentence makes even this world of memory recede behind the general aim of the group, to which the narrator returns "in some
valley or another," listening to their League songs and camping
opposite the tent of their leader. The journey into memory is
only a part of the greater journey to the unknown. Continuously
and consistently, reality is superseded by fancy, and past and
present are merged in gentle irony. "The peacocks screeched
in the garden, and Louis conversed in Spanish with Puss-in-

Boots, while Hans Resom [-Moser], who was shaken after his peeps into the masquerade of life, took a vow of pilgrimage to the tomb of Charlemagne" (VI, 25).

This style is properly described as magic and reminds us that, in his most inspired moments, Hesse did not want to be called a poet or an artist, but a magician. *Childhood of a Magician* (*Kindheit des Zauberers*, 1937) was the title of one of his autobiographical ventures (IV, 449–468). Another followed the model of Jean Paul's famous *Conjectural Biography* and contained the confession: "The magic conception of life had always appealed to me, I had never been a 'modern man,' and I had believed that Hoffmann's *Golden Pot* and especially, of course, [Novalis'] *Heinrich von Ofterdingen* were more valuable textbooks than all the histories of the world and of nature" (IV, 485).

Hesse wondered whether he could attain the merit of these books or even surpass them. But "if my own artistic dreams had been a delusion, and if I was incapable of a *Golden Pot* or a *Magic Flute*, I still had been born a magician. Since a long time I had advanced far enough on the Eastern path of Lao-tse and of the *I Ching*, so I knew exactly how accidental and changeable was this so-called reality" (IV, 486–487). "I remembered the Chinese prescription, stood still for one whole minute with suppressed breath, and became disconnected from the delusion of reality. . . . Greatly embarrassed, the watchmen were left behind" (IV, 489).

12 · The Serenity of Faith

FOR A LONG TIME Hesse had observed the development of a dangerous political climate in Germany, in which no failure or mistake was admitted. Everything was blamed on the outside world. Nobody had heeded the advice given in *Zarathustra's Return*, to accept Germany's fate as meaningful. The developments after 1933 were followed by Hesse from a distance, with disapproval and disgust. The speeches of Hitler and his ministers and the Nazi newspapers and pamphlets affected him like poison gas. A wave of meanness, lying, and astute ambitiousness created an air that he could not breathe. As he wrote in a letter to Rudolf Pannwitz in 1955, he "did not need the massive atrocities which only years later became known. This poison gas, this desecration of language and debasement of truth was entirely sufficient to push me again to the brink of the abyss where I had been during the war years [from 1914 to 1918]. The air was foul again, life had once more become questionable" (*Briefe*. Enlarged edition, 1964, p. 437).

Nevertheless, Hesse refrained from political action and did not sign any intellectual manifestos against Nazi Germany. He was opposed to all changes by force, even if they appeared to be justifiable. He did not believe that killings and shootings could make man better. A better world could be reached only by the turn inward.

This attitude was by no means synonymous with escapism or cowardice. When Hitler's assumption of power led to the expulsion of nonconformists and of Jewish writers, Hesse as a matter of course gave shelter to the pursued. From the first year of the brown terror, writers of different persuasions were welcomed in the Casa Rossa, to relax and to find help and assistance. Thomas Mann arrived in March 1933 and became an intimate friend. In 1950 Hesse, in retrospect, called their friendship one of the most satisfactory and frictionless of his life and described it as miraculous that two writers of such different antecedents and styles could meet in the cool air of cosmopolitanism.

Another welcome guest was the Chassidic philosopher Martin Buber, whom Hesse had admired for many years as one of the most valuable personalities of contemporary literature. (In 1949 he would propose Buber for the Nobel prize in literature.)

Buber was followed in 1935 by the radical Swabian theologian Christoph Schrempf, who had translated Kierkegaard and had left the Protestant church because of religious differences. Hesse held long disputations with the spirited old man and, after his death, wrote a touching eulogy (IV, 768–779). And so the stream of refugees continued. None of them, however, was able to draw Hesse into a literary clique. He remained the great individualist and joined no other literary organization after his resignation from the Prussian Academy of Letters.

Hesse's identification with the opposition took other paths. During the Nazi years he wrote articles for the *Neue Zürcher Zeitung*. He also contributed articles to the leading Swedish literary digest, *Bonniers Litterära Magasin*, which in 1935–36 brought them out in translation. They were independent reviews of everything new and good in the German language, wherever it was published. Hesse was among the first who really appreciated Robert Musil and Kafka, just as Kafka had appreciated those of Hesse's books that were published during his lifetime. Special efforts were devoted to the discussion of books suppressed or deliberately neglected by the Nazi regime, books by Jews and Catholics, and books which other critics found too hot to handle.

Hesse's views were attacked not only by the Nazis, but also by some emigrants, who thought that he should not have mentioned books still published in Germany. But he did mention them if they appeared valuable to him. After the middle of the nineteen-thirties, Hesse gave up public reviewing because it interfered with the writing of his final novel, *The Bead Game*.

Hesse's earlier writings were at first left alone by the Nazis, though they were not recommended. When he was asked to revise his essay A *Library of the World's Literature* (*Eine Bibliothek der Weltliteratur* (1929) in keeping with Nazi directives, he indignantly refused to do so (VII, 582–583). Of his other works published in Germany, Hesse was able to sell almost half a million copies, fourteen times as much as he was selling in Switzerland. This fact proved to him the continued existence of a cosmopolitan and liberal Germany in the face of all the terror and suppression.

Naturally, Hesse's political disengagement made him officially suspect, and in later years printing paper was not allotted to him for new editions of his works. He also was singled out for attacks by the monthly *Neue Literatur* and by *Das Schwarze Korps*, the organ of the storm troopers, and was called a traitor because of the literary articles he had published in Sweden. He protested vigorously in the *Neue Literatur* that he was of Swiss nationality and therefore not obligated to obey any code intended for Germans.

Yet the writing of fiction remained Hesse's favorite method of opposition, and his last great novel was intended partly as a rallying point against the forces of barbarism. In *The Bead Game* (1943) he sought to build up a spiritual atmosphere in which he could live and breathe and express the resistance of the spirit. He felt also that it might strengthen his German friends in their endurance.

The Bead Game (Das Glasperlenspiel, 1943), or *Magister Ludi*, as it is called in English, formed the core of Hesse's production from 1931 to 1942. Its first chapters appeared in Martin Bodmer's and Herbert Steiner's *Corona* and in Samuel Fischer's *Neue Rundschau*. As early as 1935 Hesse called it the final goal of his life and poetic activity. But its gestation was slow. Pauses of six months to a year interrupted the writing process. Meanwhile, *Hours in My Garden* was published in 1936. Yet Hesse kept on, finishing his manuscript on April 29, 1942. It was sent immediately to Peter Suhrkamp, Samuel

Fischer's successor, who tried to bring the book out in Germany, but had to give up the attempt after seven months. It was therefore printed in Switzerland, and only a few copies succeeded in crossing the border.

After the collapse of his pride and the merciless reckoning evident in *Steppenwolf*, Hesse endeavored to gain a new relation to reality. *Narcissus and Goldmund* as well as *The Journey to the East* conceived of life as a symbol. Man was called upon to change unrelenting lower reality into transparent higher reality. However, there were so many ways of living one's life: there were riddles and contradictions, and the image was lacking in unity. It was this unity which Hesse tried to visualize in *The Bead Game*.

He was generally inspired by an episode from Goethe's novel *Wilhelm Meisters Wanderjahre*, 1821–1829 (translated by Thomas Carlyle as Wilhelm Meister's Years of Travel), known as the "pedagogical province." Here too boys are educated in an ideal college community supervised by sage masters. Goethe's institution is also situated in Switzerland (as was its historical model, the Fellenberg Academy). Goethe's acolytes are initiated into a very new relation to God and the world and are supposed to form the nucleus of a better future. But aside from general similarities, special points of contact are lacking. Although Hesse venerated Goethe, he did not accept him without criticism and was aware of their differences (cf. also IV, 266–267; 285–286). Hesse's novel stands on its own feet and must be judged independently of any predecessors.

While Goethe's pedagogical province was designed as a reform community presaging a coming humanity, Hesse begins his story after his academy has been in operation for some time or, more precisely, after it has developed some signs of age and decay. Castalia, as he calls his institution, received its name from the spring at the southern slope of Mount Parnassus, which was sacred to the Muses.

Castalia was originally meant as a cure for the ills of modern pluralistic civilization. Modern "journalistic" multifariousness called for some central frame of reference which would restore and insure the unity of culture or, if necessary, would even develop it. This unity would derive from the trans-

cendental harmony of the Divine, where all human thoughts
and actions find their ultimate meaning. But since man is forever removed from God, he can attain the ultimate only in
symbolic form. This form is embodied in the bead game, a game
played with glass beads strung on wires, with each bead repre-
senting a special theme or idea.

The symbolic character of the bead game becomes clear
from the secrecy surrounding it. Its content is never spelled out
in logical exactness, but is only indicated by generalized hints.
Individual cultural activities or ideas are understood in their
peculiar structure, and an attempt is made to combine them
and to seek higher structural connections. Things are set in
proper perspective and are recognized in their transcendental
relationship. They become translucent glass beads which anticipate the cosmic unity meant by the deity. The dreams of the
subconscious are correlated to the abstractions of the intellect;
the revelations of art to the systems of philosophy; romantic
and Platonic visions to Chinese and Indian speculations;
Nicholas of Cusa to Leibnitz and Hegel.

The idea is to pursue the disparate elements of modern
culture, and of every culture, to a common divine fountainhead.
The bead game is no mere sport for jaded intellectuals. It might
be described as an Asiatic idea, as an occidental counterpiece
of the Indian *Tat twam asi*. For in Hesse's view, the elements of
culture are by no means unimportant. They are not the inconsequential veil of Maya, but retain their weight and individuality. In fact, they retain it far more than in *Siddhartha*, where
a certain passivity is discernible in Siddhartha's attempt to live
a life of usefulness. This time Hesse wants to live life in earnest
and find an applicable and practical solution for the problem
of human existence. The pedagogues of Castalia are to educate
other pedagogues and finally to reshape the world through
them.

These pedagogues are organized in a community; all are
unmarried and have no worldly possessions. They can, however,
resign from the order if they are later attracted by a more
worldly life. The order has separate organizations in every
country, and each of its provinces has its own hierarchy. The

highest office of every province is that of the *Glasperlenspiel-meister*, the Magister Ludi, under whose direction are twelve music masters who assist him in the selection and instruction of novices. The order is supervised by the state, which for its own benefit has here created a realm of creativity free from political interference.

This new institution of higher learning works in close contact with the ordinary educational agencies and even provides some of their teachers and scholars. But its aim is not primarily utilitarian. It is responsible for culture as a whole, not merely for education, or scholarship, or fine arts, or music. The harmony of culture is brought out in public performances of a solemn, festival character.

Our age has witnessed a decline of truly universal education in many countries in favor of narrowly specialized and utilitarian training. Hesse's idea is therefore understandable when one interprets it as a revival of classical German Humanism or even of Wilhelm von Humboldt's old university idea, which was the opposite of a conglomeration of special schools. Indeed, the Latin language plays a large part in the educational system of Hesse's order. And like the humanists, Hesse wanted to put the specializations of modern life into their proper perspective by fostering an insight into their mutual interdependence.

Yet the idea of the novel is not anthropocentric. Wilhelm Meister's motto "Remember to live!" cannot be said to be the motto of Josef Knecht, who in the end dies a sacrificial death. On the contrary, the Castalian game is clearly theocentric. All the analogies and correspondences of the bead game represent the "Unio Mystica of all the separate members of the Universitas Litterarum" (VI, 109) and are an inadequate ideogram of the faithfully visualized *numen*.

Another factor precluding any interpretation on the basis of humanistic idealism is the time setting of the novel. In it, we are transported to the year 2400 A.D. The bead game is in its decline and is no longer a guide to the cultural future. The philosophical content of the game is no longer manifested in live images, but in the abstract allegories of an esoteric sect.

This esoteric character of the bead game in its decline at

once becomes clear from the abstract and circumstantial style
in which the idea of service and of individual dedication is
described in the opening sentences of the story:

It is our intention to preserve in this book the meagre amounts of
biographical material that we have been able to discover in regard
to Josef Knecht, the Ludi Magister Josephus III, as he is called
in the annals of the Bead Game. We are not blind to the fact that
this attempt somehow contradicts the prevailing laws and customs
of spiritual culture or at least appears to do it. For the very extinction of all individual traits, the almost perfect absorption of the
individual by the hierarchy of the educational system and the
sciences and humanities is one of the ruling principles of our
spiritual culture. And accordingly this principle in a long tradition
has been put into practice to such a degree that today it is extremely
difficult and in many cases even completely impossible to discover
biographical and psychological details about individuals who have
served this hierarchy in an important manner; in many cases not
even the personal names can any longer be traced. It belongs after
all to the characteristics of the spiritual culture of our province that
its hierarchic organisation follows the ideal of anonymity and approaches very closely the realization of this ideal (VI, 80).

If the ideal were still understood, such a lengthy and detailed explanation would no longer be necessary. Its hopeful
warmth has gone, abstract words like "material," "annals," "laws
and customs," "hierarchy," and "principles" have replaced the
concrete images of the world. Qualifying expressions like "somehow," "almost," "to a degree," "in many cases," "after all," and
"very closely," make the statements less obligatory. Involved
sentences with their dependent clauses betray a hesitant, roundabout way of ratiocination.

The twelve music masters of the order are always aware of
the dangers threatening their ideal and are therefore constantly
looking for promising disciples who are not yet lost in abstractions. One of them, the Old Music Master, comes to an ordinary
school where a boy by the name of Josef Knecht has displayed
an unusual gift for music and a very healthy industry toward
learning. He examines Josef and finds him not only gifted but
modest. Josef is able to forget himself entirely in his music and
can therefore understand music as a representation of the cosmic
harmony. On the strength of his gifts and his character, he is
selected to attend one of the order's boarding schools.

With Josef Knecht's entry into the story, the style becomes more concrete. The Escholz School, to which he is sent at first, is depicted accurately in a series of succinct, direct statements:

> Escholz was the largest and most recent one of Castalia's boarding schools. All its buildings were modern. No city was close by, only a small village-like settlement. Behind it the institution unfolded its complex serenely on a wide plain around a big, open, rectangular field, in the midst of which five mammoth trees raised their dark cones like the number five on a die. The large field was partly covered with turf and partly with sand and was only interrupted by two big swimming pools with flowing water, to which broad, flat steps were leading down (VI, 139).

From Escholz, Josef Knecht moves to Waldzell, the place of higher education dominating the whole "pedagogical province" (this term, taken from Goethe, is employed for Castalia; VI, 134). Here Knecht's studies are still regulated in a college-oriented way. In Waldzell his fellow-student Plinio Designori, scion of a ruling family, "de signori," of the country, and not like Josef a mere servant, a "Knecht," becomes most important to him. Plinio is a gifted young man destined for a career in business or politics, who will not become a member of the elite order of the bead game players. For Knecht, Plinio represents "the world," against which he has to defend "the spirit." But in defending it, Knecht receives an insight into the role of the spirit in life as a whole.

Spiritual exercises must never become an irresponsible sport, but must lead to meditation about the proper meaning of life. The spirit must not set itself up in haughty seclusion, but must assume a guiding and regulating function. Although Plinio intends to return to practical life, he does not merely want to amuse himself at Waldzell with intellectual games. He desires to become acquainted with that higher sphere which gives meaning and direction to practical life.

That the Castalian spirit does not lead an ivory tower existence is also emphasized after Knecht's graduation from Waldzell, when he achieves full freedom of choice in his studies. The Waldzell graduates are not given to athletic excesses or sexual promiscuousness. However, they do not shun sport altogether, and they are not restricted in their relations

with girls. "In regard to women the Castalian students anticipate neither marriage with its temptations and dangers, nor
are they familiar with the prudishness of so many previous
epochs, which either forced the students to asceticism or referred them more or less to prostitutes and women of easy
virtue" (VI, 188). Marriage and return to practical life are not
prohibited, and temporary love affairs are permissible. When
a Castalian student becomes an ascetic, he does so of his own
free will, and only because the exigencies of spiritual existence
cause him to give up worldly ties. For spiritual culture remains
Castalia's primary concern.

Knecht is initiated into the principles of the bead game by
Master Fritz Tegularius. He learns regulated meditation in order
to gain poise and a sense of proportion, distance, and wisdom.
He continues to practice the music of the great classical masters,
from Purcell to Bach and Mozart. Music expresses the basic
unity of the universe by dissolving its contrapuntal differences
into transcending harmony. The romantic music of *Gertrude*,
which reminded one of Brahms and Max Reger, if not of
Chopin, is no longer important. Even Beethoven is shunned,
since he stands at the beginnings of Romanticism (cf. also IV,
401–402). And the stridencies of jazz, which played such a part
in *Steppenwolf*, have receded to past history together with the
whole belletristic age.

The highest wisdom is transmitted to Knecht by the so-
called Older Brother, a hermit living in an artificial bamboo
grove, in the manner of Chinese sages. Through him, Knecht
is initiated into the intricacies of the sixty-four hexagrams of
the Confucian *I Ching* (3000 B.C.), which are composed of
broken weak lines and uninterrupted strong lines. The weak
lines represent the female principle of Yin, and the strong lines
the male principle of Yang, and Yin and Yang, fluid and solid,
darkness and light comprise the whole of creation.

Such geometric-magical configurations were of course also
visualized by the Pythagoreans, by the Platonic Academy, and
by German Romanticists like Novalis. Thus, by means of the
Chinese philosophical symbols, Hesse is returning to one of
the most persistent traditions of the occidental spirit. The

setting for this philosophical experience is of Chinese and likewise occidental preciseness:

> It was late afternoon when he reached the bamboo grove. He entered and to his astonishment saw a Chinese pavilion standing in the center of a strange garden, a spring was bubbling from a wooden pipe. The water flowed into a bed of pebbles and filled a masonry basin nearby, in the chinks of which green plants were growing and in whose clear and quiet waters swam a few golden carps (VI, 206).

This description consists of neatly arranged principal clauses and pays close attention to visual detail.

The same spiritual sobriety is also transmitted to Knecht through his long association with Peter Jacobus of Mariafels, to whom he is sent to study history. He is to learn of man's extension into the past and thus into all of human society. Pater Jacobus is the living embodiment of the hierarchic world of the Middle Ages, and he makes Josef Knecht intimately acquainted with the European past. But although Josef appreciates his wonderfully disciplined world, he does not become a Benedictine. The chief result of Knecht's sojourn at Mariafels is his realization that history represents an important reality, with problems of its own that are worthy of positive solution. He can therefore consent to the order's employment of him as a political emissary: he is chosen to gain the Benedictines' approval for permanent diplomatic representation of Castalia at the Vatican.

At the end of his long years of apprenticeship, Knecht is ready to take over the highest office of the order. He becomes Magister Ludi under the name of Josephus III. For a while he does his best to revive the old Castalian idea of the spirit as a guiding principle for human culture. But then he realizes that his efforts are futile and that Castalia is succumbing to the old intellectual temptation to become abstract and esoteric.

The esoteric intellect is personified by Knecht's erstwhile teacher Fritz Tegularius.

> Tegularius was a precursor like most lonely geniuses. He actually lived in a Castalia which did not yet exist, but could come into existence tomorrow, in a Castalia even more secluded from the

world, inwardly degenerating by the aging and loosening of the meditative moral of the order, in a world, in which the loftiest flights of the spirit and the most exclusive devotion to sublime values were still possible, but where a neatly developed and free-wheeling spirituality had no other aims than the private enjoyment of its highly cultivated abilities (VI, 368).

These abstract nouns, participial constructions, and involved sentences betray the impending danger. Tegularius' intellectualism is extremely abstract, with no involvement in common reality. He considers human history an unworthy study. His days are filled by the search for cultural parallels and the discovery of witty correspondences. For him the bead game has become an irresponsible aesthetic pastime, and metaphysical contemplation is mere romantic self-enjoyment. He fails to see that genuine knowledge must affirm the unity of the world and must therefore lead to the service of his fellow man.

Knecht now understands why the old music master so often directed his attention to Buddha who, unlike his disciples, did not remain lost in contemplation but returned to the world to preach salvation. He too finally sees no other way out but to leave the order and to resume a personal responsibility for reality. When he discloses his intentions to Master Alexander, the chairman of the order's board of directors, the state of things is revealed in a very circumstantial style in which the abstractness of the later Castalia is emphasized by a difficult sentence construction, and by the employment of the subjunctive, thus bringing in an element of unreality and lack of commitment.

That Master Knecht with his model obedience, his fine, cultured behavior, his modesty and his tact would be able one day to visit him without previous announcement, to resign from his office arbitrarily and without previous consultation with his superiors, and would in this revolting manner completely disregard all customs and traditions, he would have believed utterly impossible (VI, 499).

The immediate purpose of Knecht's resignation is to dedicate himself to the education of Tito Designori, the son of his old friend Plinio. Plinio, after his attendance at the famous schools, held a high position in the political world, where he also met with the common disappointments of reality. He now wants to give to his son Tito more than a practical education

and sends him to Knecht to be instructed in Castalian principles. Tito likewise has a brilliant mind and does not readily
submit to Castalian aloofness. Josef Knecht wrestles with him
for his young soul, but finally sees that he has to meet the
challenge directly in the world of "lower" reality. Truth exists,
to be sure, but it cannot be caught in a perfect system. It can
only be approached by a perfection of one's self. Truth wants
to be lived.

With Knecht's resignation from the decaying order, the
original Castalian idea is restored, and the hope for a victory
of the spirit over the forces of barbarism is revived. Hesse's
style expresses this in colorful images which are arranged in
paratactical clauses, rich in musical triads:

> Before him lay the small lake, grayish green and without ripples;
> on its distant shore was a steep, high, rocky slope, with a sharp,
> serrated rim gutting into the thin, greenish, cool morning sky, cold
> in forbidding shadows. Yet behind this rim the sun had risen, its
> light was reflected here and there in the tiny splinters of a sharp
> stone edge. Only minutes were lacking until above the mountain
> jags the sun would appear and would flood with light the lake and
> the elevated valley. Attentively and in a reflecting mood Knecht
> was observing the image, whose stillness, seriousness, and beauty
> he felt to be unfamiliar and yet affecting him and exhorting him.
> Stronger than during yesterday's ride he was sensing the weight,
> the coolness, and the dignified aloofness of the high mountain
> world, which does not meet man half-way, does not invite him,
> barely tolerates him. And it appeared to him strangely meaningful
> that his first step into the new freedom of worldly life had led him
> exactly here, into this quiet and cold greatness (VI, 537).

This scenic description contains all the observation of natural
details; the nouns and adjectives are carefully chosen for their
exact shade of meaning. Yet, an element of transcendency enters
by the stress upon the "unfamiliar" "stillness, seriousness, and
beauty" of the view and "the weight, the coolness, and the
dignified aloofness of the high mountain world." The passage
presents no self-contained picture; the view is "strangely meaningful" and thus becomes transparent. In such passages the
style of *The Bead Game* reaches its perfection.

A transparent world is no accidental array of realistic details to which one has to adapt by compromise. It demands

commitment. When Tito challenges his teacher to show by
physical prowess that life for him is more than intellectual
shadow-boxing, Knecht accepts this challenge in spite of his age
and in spite of every sane hygienic precaution. He cannot disap-
point this boy who believes in him. Knecht hurls himself into
the icy mountain lake and dies. His death is a sacrifice to the
boy's soul (VII, 640), although this is not clearly expressed and
although other possible meanings are admitted by the deliberate
clouding of Knecht's intentions. In any case he has proved to
his charge that he meant what he preached, and has thus ful-
filled his mission. Tito will continue where his teacher has left
off, and Knecht will live on in his work. Man's spirit is inde-
structible and immortal. (Hesse never believed in personal,
bodily resurrection.)

Castalia's meaning as an initiation into a life of service is
further emphasized by the three imaginative biographies ap-
pended to the main story. Like Jean Paul's appendices, they
add no foreign material, but represent necessary variations of
the main theme. But even more than that, they are transposi-
tions of Knecht's story into former times, thus extending his self
by the detailing of former incarnations. Hesse himself stated that
he believed these imaginative biographies "to be perhaps the
most valuable part of our book" (VI, 192). They demonstrate
the timeless tradition with which he wanted to oppose the chaos
of modern barbarism. They also make time relative and show
that present, past, and future always coexist in man's soul.

The basis for these stories is provided by a concept of reincarnation, which only loosely corresponds to its Hindu counterpart. Man here is reincarnated in different human forms in
order to find the best opportunity to reach perfection. A single
life does not suffice. Thus man must step from one life into
the other (cf. also the poem "Stufen" ["Steps"], VI, 555–
556). This idea was first expressed in Lessing's treatise on *The
Education of Mankind*, with which Hesse can be assumed to
have been familiar. His concept of progressive reincarnation
differs greatly from the Hindu view of an ever-recurrent circle
of reincarnations (including possible animal reincarnations)
directed by karma, which for a Buddhist can be broken only by

a strict withdrawal from every earthly attachment. But it agrees with the optimistic concept of reincarnation as expressed by the Chinese Chuang-tzu. It is not the only instance which shows Hesse as having overcome his earlier fascination for Indian philosophy in favor of Chinese conceptions. In Chinese Universism he found a system more closely related to his thinking than were the systems of Christian theology. For here too man's way to immortality was a direct way, and did not presuppose a break or catastrophe.

Altogether, Knecht's self is led through four forms of existence, with the last one comprising the main body of the novel. His first form is that of the Rain Maker who, in prehistoric times, functioned as the esteemed magician of the tribe. Living in complete harmony with nature he has practised magical incantations in a spirit of veneration. But one day the gods deny the plea for rain, and the magician thereupon offers himself as a sacrifice for the tribal community. His life has been one of service in the first stage of man's development, the stage of complete harmony with nature and unquestioned acceptance of its laws.

The second story, "The Father Confessor," concerns the second form, when doubt and despair have set in and destroyed the primitive harmony. Hesse had already used Old Christian surroundings in the *Three Legends from Thebaid,* which he published in 1935 (II, 637–660). In "The Father Confessor," Josef Knecht is living in the period of the Old Christian Anchorites as "Josephus Famulus." He runs away from his clerical office in the awareness of his own sinfulness and is then strengthened in his faith by Dion, his father confessor. Yet even Dion displays a disturbing uncertainty. When Josephus has mastered his impulses and returned to his office, he continues to serve the community, but is still convinced of his unworthiness. Dion hopes that the practice of love may make him worthier.

In the third story, "Indian Biography," renewed hope has seized the hero, who is called Dasa (an Indian translation of the German "Knecht"). Here we have average man who hopes to redeem himself by obeying rules and commandments. The

youth Dasa has grown up in the country and now wants to go
out into the world. A hermit lets him experience his future
life in a brief, magical dream.

Dasa will become a king, but in order to protect his country
and his son he will wage war, and will be defeated. Thus his
righteousness will avail him nothing, and earthly happiness will
prove an illusion. Full of horror the youth awakens and realizes
that "everything was nothing—no, not nothing, it was Maya"
(VI, 682). Therefore Dasa renounces the world and practises
mystic meditation like the saintly hermit. He thus overcomes
worldly temptations by concentrating on the universal unity of
things and affirming its existence without resistance. Yet this
self-centered withdrawal from the world was never satisfactory
for a man of Hesse's Christian background.

In the third, as well as in the second, stage of Knecht's
reincarnation, the practice of love in the sense of Christian
charity has played an important part, and in the fourth story,
i.e., in the body of the novel, the problem of reshaping the world
and contributing to more than personal redemption occupies
the main space.

Knecht does not reject creation as senseless Maya, but tries
to transform it into a symbol of God in terms of the Castalian
idea. True piety requires a feeling of responsibility for the
world, and Knecht unflinchingly accepts his share in God's
work. He does not thereby become a saint immediately, but is
on his way to the sainthood which would be the consummation
of Hesse's ideal. But only God's grace can place man among
the "Immortals," as they are called in *Steppenwolf*. As long
as man is alive, he can fulfill his mission only by a personal
dedication to the spirit. The moral of *The Bead Game* calls
for a personal effort. Salvation depends on the individual. Hesse
has presented no panacea; only a hope for betterment.

The three imaginative biographies are more easily accepted
by the average reader than is the story itself. Occupied with
historical and regional realities, they achieve the enviable status
of colorful symbols. It is the main body of the book that is
more difficult to appreciate. Castalia's world is strangely emas-
culated, and for long stretches we move in a rarified atmosphere.
The story deals with intellectual abstractions and esoteric

ritualisms that have lost their meaning, and the style often becomes unavoidably allegorical. But there is the other world where symbols are alive, the world of the Older Brother and of Pater Jacobus, the world of Plinio, and finally, of Knecht himself.

The wonderful scenic descriptions should warn the reader not to take the abstract mechanisms of Castalia in its decline too seriously. Abstract passages were necessary, but they were not written by an author whose powers were on the wane. When the style of *The Bead Game* was uneven, it was intentionally so. As Hesse had said already in 1909, "We 'narrators of today' practice an art of the day after tomorrow, the stylistic laws of which do not yet exist" (*Neue Rundschau*, XX [1909], 782).

Hesse was not the only modern author who was accused of intellectual dryness. Similar objections were raised against Thomas Mann's *Magic Mountain* (1924), which was likewise concerned with man's role in the world of culture and ended in showing us Hans Castorp actively participating in life. Hesse was thoroughly aware of the general similarity of Mann's approach and could therefore raise his friend to the dignity of a Magister Ludi under the name of Thomas von der Trave. (Lübeck on the Trave River was Mann's birthplace.) He became Knecht's predecessor in the highest office of the order, which also implies a certain criticism. For in the last analysis, Mann's vision of the future was merely a humanistic vision, as the example of his *Joseph* cycle shows clearly. The sphere of mystic intuition was foreign to Mann.

When *The Bead Game* arrived in Thomas Mann's Pasadena study, Mann was occupied with the writing of *Dr. Faustus*. *The Bead Game* impressed him as a "wonderfully mature and rich novel" and a "well-rounded masterpiece" (Letter of April 4, 1945). He was startled by the similarity of their two conceptions. His *Dr. Faustus* was also a fictional biography; it too gave a prominent place to music; and it too criticized modern civilization. But while Hesse referred to the depravity of the age in general terms, Mann was concerned primarily with its German manifestations. His strength lay in the analysis of the spreading chaos, and his demonic musician Adrian Leverkühn was a protagonist of an art which Hesse would have termed *Musik des Untergangs* (music of decay).

Mann therefore ended on a note of profound pessimism. Hesse, on the other hand, saw beyond the chaos and visualized a renewed culture. In spite of all its seriousness, his work was still filled with serenity. This serenity found expression in a relatively simple style, while Mann's skepticism produced a style of many hedgings and reverses. But the author of *Steppenwolf* was surely able to understand why his distinguished contemporary could be no naive idealist.

Thomas Mann was not the only contemporary appearing in disguise in *The Bead Game*. As in *The Journey to the East*, Hesse introduced many of his friends by their Latinized or Romanized names. His friends Franz Schall and Josef Feinhals became Clangor and Collofino, and his musically gifted nephew Carlo Isenberg became Carlo Ferromonte, an organist and connoisseur of old music. Heinrich Perrot, the Calw master craftsman, was introduced as Bastian Perrot. These and other such allusions were part of Hesse's methods for making the bead-game world transparent and for suspending the rationalistic borderline between reality and fancy. It is not necessary to understand all of these allusions, so long as one shares in the feeling that Castalia does not lie entirely on the moon.

Two important characters have their prototypes in history. Pater Jacobus is modeled after the great historian Jakob Burckhardt, who also led a monkish existence. Mariazell, where Pater Jacobus is in charge of the archives, is a counterpart of the famous Benedictine abbey of Mariä Einsiedeln, where Dr. Lang received his undergraduate training. Knecht's "erstwhile teacher" Tegularius represents Hesse's former teacher Nietzsche (if we are to believe Joseph Mileck). He has the same aversion to history as Nietzsche himself. But the name "Tegularius" is Latin for "Ziegler" ("Tiler") and may also remind one of the *Man Named Ziegler* (*Ein Mensch mit Namen Ziegler*, 1908) from the *Fabulierbuch* (Book of Fables, 1935; II, 892–897), a very correct gentleman adoring a science which he does not understand. Or could Tegularius have anything to do with Hesse's fellow Swabians, the humanistic philosopher Theobald

Ziegler (1846–1918) or the more independent thinker Leopold Ziegler (1881–1958)? Perhaps this secret can still be lifted.

The meaning of Knecht's own name is obvious. However, *Knecht* in German means more than "menial servant." Through its etymological connection with *knight* it also carries the connotation of noble faithfulness. *Knecht Ruprecht* is one of the German equivalents of our *Santa Claus*; he is a servant of the Savior. Knecht in *The Bead Game* develops into a servant of God, and his service becomes a form of worship. He literally follows the Christian command to love one's neighbor. "God is love, and he that dwelleth in love, dwelleth in God, and God in him" (I. Joh. IV, 16). At the same time Knecht's given name Josef recalls the biblical Jacob's favorite son Joseph who was rejected by his brothers and then became a powerful official at the court of the Pharaoh. *Josef* points out that this *Knecht* belongs to the blessed poor that have been elected.

The form of Hesse's religion is individualistic and Protestant, but not wholly so. This has already been suggested by the dedication of the book "To the Travelers to the East." Knecht for a long time is an organization man, and the monkish order of the *Glasperlenspieler* with its peculiar rituals serves as a substitute for a church. That the problem of the religious community really occupied Hesse's mind was also indicated by Knecht's long stay in the Benedictine monastery and his interest in the Catholic Church (cf. also VII, 374). But in the end even the order was deserted in favor of a personal commitment to the service of truth. Knecht, as well as his author, wanted to be a complete personality extending his roots into the social as well as the transcendental sphere, but both refrained from the dogmatic seclusion of the *ecclesia visibilis*. Their church was the *ecclesia invisibilis* of the spirit and they never felt the need for a divine mediator in the specifically Christian sense. Christ for them was a very venerable and even heroic person, but he was not basically different from the other saints.

Between the main body of *The Bead Game* and the three conjectural biographies we find another appendix consisting of Knecht's poetic exercises. These take up a very old tradition, the tradition of didactic poetry, which can boast of such renowned practitioners as Walther von der Vogelweide, Schiller, Goethe, and Stefan George. Didactic poetry is of course anathema to all partisans of Romantic emotionalism and personal poetic expression. Hesse himself has left us so many pure lyrical gems that in his case there is no possible doubt of his poetic gifts. When he nevertheless saw fit to compose a considerable amount of didactic verse, he must have meant it as another way out of irresponsible subjectivity.

A man like Knecht who aspires to a life of service, cannot of course indulge in the mere nursing of his private moods. On the other hand, forsaking poetry altogether would have signified a withdrawal into the abstract which Knecht fought all his life. Thus he arrived at a vesting of his philosophical insight in a cloak of poetic, rythmical, and musical language. Knecht's gnomic verses are therefore more than rhymed philosophy. Apart from the main story they attest to the non-rational character of his insight and to the less than private character of his devotion. They serve to overcome the emotionalism of the nineteenth century in the direction of a new, responsible form. They express in the genre of poetry what Hesse has frequently indicated by his references to classical music, from Purcell to Mozart. Perhaps the truth of these observations is proved most succinctly by the concluding verses of the poetic appendix:

Das Glasperlenspiel
Musik des Weltalls und Musik
der Meister
Sind wir bereit in Ehrfurcht
anzuhören,
Zu reiner Feier die verehrten
Geister
Begnadeter Zeiten zu
beschwören.

Wir lassen vom Geheimnis uns
erheben
Der magischen Formelschrift,
in deren Bann
Das Uferlose, Stürmende, das
Leben,
Zu klaren Gleichnissen gerann.

The Bead Game
We are ready to listen in awe
To music of the cosmos and
music of the masters,
To call up the fortunate
centuries
For a pure festival of
spirits revered.

We let the secret uplift us
Of magical prescriptions,
in whose power
Life, and all that was boundless
and storming,
Flowed into lucid images.

Sternbildern gleich
     ertönen sie kristallen,
In ihrem Dienst ward unserm
     Leben Sinn,
Und keiner kann aus ihren
     Kreisen fallen,
Als nach der heiligen Mitte
     hin.
	Like constellations,
	     crystalline they sound,
	In whose service our lives are
	     fulfilled,
	And in their circles none can fall,
	Unless toward their sacred
	     centers.
	                    (VI, 556).

Hesse's *Bead Game* became accessible to readers within Germany only after World War II. The novel achieved an initial success with foreign readers which, however, was not maintained for long. It appeared to them as too philosophical and was at once classified as another peculiarly German educational novel. It suffered the same fate as Goethe's novel *Wilhelm Meister's Years of Travel*, which also failed to be understood as a valid aesthetic achievement, and has been misjudged even in Germany as a purely didactic piece of fiction, without the least trace of irony.

However, like *Wilhelm Meister*, Hesse's *Bead Game* seems destined to last. When its German edition appeared in 1946, it elicited more than passing interest. Although the book met with general acclaim, it also was severely criticized for its so-called "weak humanism" and its "formless" and "pedantic" language. But these criticisms were refuted by informed champions of Hesse's work, and the novel continued to affect its German readers deeply. Here was no mere criticism of culture as Mann had offered in *Dr. Faustus*. Here was a continuing and serene faith. Here also was hope and dedication to that hope. To be sure, it was hope for the individual rather than for institutions and systems. But that is the way in which changes of culture have always started. The fate of mankind, as Nietzsche has aptly observed, moves on dove's feet.

13 · The Charcoal Burner

AT THE END of World War II, Hesse's mood had become very bitter. His wife's relatives and friends had perished in Himmler's extermination camps, and he was receiving many letters that shocked him by their blindness to what had happened. Only the letters from active resistance fighters could be taken seriously, for hope lay with the few and not with the masses.

Yet these few had always counted Hesse among their spiritual guides, and they were starting to point him out again to the bewildered German nation. In 1946, the year of his Nobel award, they selected Hesse for the Goethe prize, which he accepted after some hesitation. He gave the prize money to charity. In 1947 he became an honorary citizen of Calw, the town of his birth. In 1950 he received the Raabe prize of the city of Brunswick, and in 1955, the peace prize of the German publishers. In the same year Hesse was awarded the order *Pour le mérite* for peaceful achievements, which made him one of Germany's immortals. German public opinion was indeed changing. Perhaps a better Germany was rising from the chaos after all. As much as Hesse was opposed to war and to nationalism, he did not want to erase national characteristics altogether. He loved the variegated multiplicity of nations (VII, 454). Yet he was as firmly resolved as ever to stay out of politics and continued his refusal to sign intellectual manifestos. For him, the renewal of culture would never come through declarations and organizations, but would always start from within.

During the last years of his life Hesse stayed at Montagnola most of the time. In the summer he regularly vacationed at Sils Maria in the upper Engadine, which became to him a second homeland. But he did not withdraw from the world, although it had become necessary for him to protect his privacy by discouraging the tactless approaches of curious strangers and autograph seekers. To real friends the Casa Hesse stood open as before.

In 1947 he saw Thomas Mann again after the latter's California exile, and the passing through of Martin Buber and Hans Carossa were other festive occasions. His old friend Ernst Morgenthaler came to paint Hesse's portrait. And suddenly there arrived André Gide who left quite an impression:

His was a quiet glance from a controlled face used to society and well educated. But in this glance and in the persistence with which he again and again returned to his subject, lay the great strength which was ruling his life and which had driven him to Africa and England, to Germany and Greece. This glance in its open fascination by the miracles of the world was capable of love and sympathy, but it was entirely unsentimental and in spite of all devotion had something objective. A thirst for insight was his basic motivation (*Merkur*, VI, 1952, p. 142).

Later, Gide's son-in-law translated *The Journey to the East*, arnd Gide himself introduced the translation with an essay (cf. *Le voyage en Orient*, tr. Jean Lambert. Paris: Calmann-Levy, 1948). Hesse thanked Gide in a letter in which he called him "a loving defender of freedom, of personality, of perseverance, of individual responsibility" (VII, 775). Another welcome guest was Peter Suhrkamp, the heir of his old publisher Samuel Fischer. Suhrkamp brought out the six volumes of Hesse's collected works for the author's seventy-fifth birthday in 1952. In 1957 he aded a seventh volume culled from Hesse's political and literary essays as well as from his letters and diaries. When Peter Suhrkamp died in 1959, Hesse expressed his admiration for him as a representative of the "true" or "genuine" or "secret" Germany.

As early as 1946, Hesse complained of the onset of old age, of progressive hardening of the arteries, and of a diminishing blood supply to his brain. "But all these evils have also their good side: One does no longer react to everything, one fails to hear many things, one does not feel some of the blows or needle stings at all, and a part of the character that was called Ego, is already there where soon the whole will be" (VII, 453). For reasons of health Hesse was unable to travel to Sweden to receive in person the Nobel prize, for which he had been selected in 1946. In his answer to the Swedish committee he emphasized his intention of continuing to serve the causes of international peace and reconciliation. At the same time he accepted the prize as an acknowledgment of the German contribution to culture.

The Nobel prize was not the only sign of Hesse's growing international fame. *Peter Camenzind, Demian,* and *Steppenwolf* had found their way into many European tongues soon after their publication. Some translations of these and other early works had also been published in the Argentine, in China, Israel, Mexico, and the United States. *Rosshalde* had reached Dutch and Russian readers. Translations of *Gertrude* were published in Sweden, the Netherlands, the United States and, much later, in Yugoslavia. After Hesse received the Nobel prize, new translations of *The Bead Game* made it an international success. And his international success was by no means short-lived or sensational. The nine translations of *Siddhartha* into Indian dialects began to appear from 1953, and *Schön ist die Jugend* (Beautiful Youth) was translated into Korean as late as 1959.)

The most astonishing echo however came from Japan, where *Siddhartha* was first translated in 1925. *The Turn Inward* appeared there in 1933. But the real vogue started in 1949 with *Demian* and *Thanks to Goethe* (*Dank an Goethe,* 1932). Since then, every work of Hesse has found its way into Japanese, and he has become a pronounced favorite of Japanese readers. By 1962 no less than seventy-five single editions of his books had appeared in Japan, and two entirely separate translations of Hesse's collected works were available. (See also VII, 875.)

The American vogue started with *Magister Ludi* (*The Bead Game*) in 1949 and led to a number of new and revised editions of books already available in English translation. Discussions of *Steppenwolf,* of *Siddhartha,* of *The Journey to the East* have become commonplace in American intellectual circles, although Hesse's fame cannot be said to have approached that of Thomas Mann or Franz Kafka.

The gestation of *The Bead Game* was interrupted by the idyl *Hours in My Garden* (*Stunden im Garten*, 1936); it was later illustrated by the graphic artist Gunter Böhmer. In this small hexametric idyl Hesse described in loving detail the terraces of his subtropical garden in Montagnola.

Dressed in a light summer suit and a gardener's straw hat he was wont to spend his forenoons in weeding and pruning. It was a resumption of the Gaienhofen garden work in a slightly altered mood. Instead of going back to nature Hesse now experienced unity in nature. Occasionally his Siamese cat Löwe came to visit and observe him, and at other times Hesse himself watched the people passing by the lower end of his garden. At noon he usually lighted a fire and sat down before this symbol of the changing of multiplicity into unity.

The author kept faith with ancient alchemistic meditations and liked to prepare special soils in the old-fashioned manner of "burning," so that his wife named him "the charcoal burner." In these meditations before the fire, Hesse played the Bead Game in his own manner by letting his mind wander among the beloved melodies of Mozart and other old masters and among related themes from prized literary and philosophical works. God permitted him

Not in our days merely to live, but often to hold
All time in suspension and to breathe timeless space. Once this was
      highly treasured—
Called removal from self, transfiguration, or holy madness.
Now it means nothing to moderns; for time is considered too costly,
And contempt of time a vice. . . . (V, 344–345).

Hesse's other idyl, *The Lame Boy* (*Der lahme Knabe*), was published in 1937 and told of a hunchback who had been his fishing companion during a few summers of his childhood. From him the author learned patience, and with him he discussed death for the first time.

Hesse's last years after *The Bead Game* were marked more by effort than by spontaneity. He had no reason to write another book. He had said all that he had intended to say, and he did not want to repeat himself. Still he was kept busy. The poet assembled earlier fairy tales and parables from the years 1910–1932 in the volume *Dream Traces* (Traumfährte, 1945), and he finally consented to the publication of his collected works in 1952. Their six volumes contained only what Hesse himself believed to be worthy of lasting attention, but the collection was far from complete. Otherwise he wrote only short tales and essays. He also published a few poems and pages from his diaries and his correspondence in private printings and in periodicals.

He edited a selection from the works of Eichendorff. He reviewed books, but only when they appeared to him especially worthwhile. Thus he was able to call attention to Anna Seghers and to Monique Saint-Helier; to the lyric poetry of Oskar Loerke and the prose essays of Peter Suhrkamp; to the masterful translations from the Chinese by Richard Wilhelm; and to the translation of the basic work of Zen Buddhism by his cousin Wilhelm Gundert. But in general, these were the years of harvesting and of restful contemplation after work well done.

Among the volumes of Hesse's collected writings, the fifth demanded special attention, as it contained the definitive collection of his poetry. Hesse had hesitated a long time before he allowed his Swiss publishers Fretz and Wasmuth to bring out a first edition of his collected poems in 1942. In subsequent editions the collection was enlarged.

By the time this collection appeared, Hesse's poems had already reached their public. Through reprints in school texts and anthologies, some of them had attained an enviable popularity. And all of his poetry had been available in some earlier collections, since Carl Busse had included Hesse's poems in the series *Neue deutsche Lyriker* (1902). But still the conclusive edition had the effect of a revelation and added measurably to Hesse's stature. It presented Hesse to many readers of *The Bead Game* in a different light.

A new lyrical personality had already been displayed in Hesse's earliest verses. Although, as a young poet Hesse had found it easy to follow the folksong tradition of German Romanticism, he soon developed his own melody. He continued the Goethean use of poetry as a great confession. *Music of the Lonely One* (Musik des Einsamen, 1915) was a revealing title.

And Romantic themes of longing homelessness and of peaceful union with nature and landscape pervaded all of Hesse's prewar poetry. Yet he treated them with an unromantic concentration on sensual detail:

Im Kastanienbaum der Wind	The wind in the chestnut tree,
Reckt verschlafen sein Gefieder,	asleep,
An den spitzen Dächern rinnt	Is shaking out his plumage,
Dämmerung und Mondschein	Twilight and moonglow seep
nieder.	Down from the points of gables.
	(Spring Night, V, 512).

The same unsentimental detachment also permitted Hesse to conjure up human figures, as exemplified by the poem "Elisabeth" (V, 443) quoted earlier in this study. One of his most impressive achievements in this genre was his "Dying Soldier" of 1915 (V, 619), which Anni Carlsson has rightfully compared to Mörike's "Deserted Maiden."

The more critical Hesse became of his Romantic sentiments, the more attention he paid to the objective human world around him, and the more he strove for the impersonal depth of Chinese poetry. The Romantic quatrains were replaced by free verse and a more involved syntax. But still Hesse could not overcome his self.

The shattering war experience led to poetic soliloquies like those contained in *Klingsor*. They were often long and reflective, averaging about thirty lines and employing iambic pentameters and tetrameters. If rhyme was present at all, it appeared in a mixed pattern. The syntax was more complex, the vocabulary more deliberate, the rhythm somewhat halting.

As a matter of fact, lyrical confessions were never completely absent from Hesse's poetry. Yet they became rarer and more detached with the years. Hesse now visualized the possibility of his own death without self-pity and melted down every evoked image in order to grasp the unity behind the variety of fleeting impressions.

There emerged a new clarity and simplicity, no longer naive, and almost brittle in its observation of distance. These mature poems still let the poetic self shine through, but the objective image now claimed the center of attention. Their quality is that of a wise serenity:

Der Blütenzweig
Immer hin und wider
Strebt der Blütenzweig im Winde
Immer auf und nieder
Strebt mein Herz gleich einem Kinde
Zwischen hellen, dunkeln Tagen,
Zwischen Wollen und Entsagen.

Bis die Blüten sind verweht
Und der Zweig in Früchten steht
Bis das Herz, der Kindheit satt
Seine Ruhe hat
Und bekennt: voll Lust und nicht vergebens
War das unruhvolle Spiel des Lebens.

The Branch of Flowers
Ever to and fro
In the wind the branch of flowers sways,
Ever up and down
My heart that is like a child sways
Between the bright and the dark days,
Between wishing and renouncing.

Until the flowers blow away
And the fruit-bearing branch stands still,
Until my heart, sated with childhood,
Takes rest
And admits: The restless game of life
Was full of joy and not for nought.

(V, 573).

In such poems the real world has become ephemeral, a shell
and a dress for the infinite. Hesse now seeks to be nothing more
than a mirror, in which passing visions and images momentarily
appear. Nature poems now occur less frequently than in his
first period, but they excel in an exactness of detail:

Durchblick ins Seetal
Zwischen grau behaarten Fichtenzweigen,
Zwischen roten, rauhen Kiefernästen,
Blauen Zedern, die sich würdig neigen,
Zwischen Lindenstämmen mit den Resten
Gelben Laubes sinkt der Blick hinunter,
Berghinab durch klamme Perspektiven,
In des Seetals freundlich-ferne Tiefen.
Sanft scheint alles dort und dennoch bunter,
Glasig schwebt der See, der licht umsäumte,

Dörfer lächeln hell mit sonnigen Dächern,
Felder wie von Malergeist geträumte
Farbenfolgen breiten sich in Fächern.

View of the Lake Valley
Between fir trees with gray, hairy needles,
Between red pine branches rough in texture,
Bluish cedars that bend with dignity,
Between linden trunks with yellow foliage
Still preserved, the view travels downward,
Down the hill through narrowing perspectives
To the friendly, deep, lake-flooded valley.
Everything seems soft there and yet brighter.
The lake hangs glassy, hemmed in by the light,
Villages with sunny roofs smile brightly,
Fields that could have formed a painting
Alternate in rows of color-sequence.

(V, 771).

And finally there emerges the philosophic clarity of *The Bead Game* poems, where Hesse tried to put into verse the pure movements of the spiritual world, the proportions of the mind and its music. The model for this poetry was provided by the fugues of Bach which can be easily discovered in long poems like "A Dream" (V, 749–752) or "Organ Playing" (V, 760–765):

Träumend und ein Lächeln auf den Lippen
Über immer zarteren Registern
Sitzt der greise Musikant, versponnen
In das Rankenwerk der Stimmengänge,
In des Fugenbaus gestufte Pfade.
Immer zarteres Filigrangestänge,
Flicht sein Spiel, mit immer dünnerem Faden
Kreuzen sich die kühnen Ornamente
Im phantastisch luftigen Tongewebe,
Immer inniger und süsser werben
Um einander die bewegten Stimmen,
Scheinen Himmelsleitern zu erklimmen,
Halten oben sich in seliger Schwebe,
Um wie Abendrosenwolken hinzusterben.

Dreaming and with lips serenely smiling,
Over ever finer tone-registers,
Sits the old musician, all enmeshed
In the tendrils of his climbing voices,
In the mounting stairs of his long fugue piece.

Ever finer filigree is added
To his play, with ever thinner threadings
He connects bold ornaments of fancy
In the airy, mirthful loom's vibrations.
Ever closer, ever sweeter wooing,
Move and mount and then recede the voices,
Seem to climb on ladders up to heaven,
Hover high as though in blissful balance,
And are fading like the clouds of evening.

(V, 763).

Hesse has in no way created new lyric forms. He was satisfied to revive existing ones and through them convey his message. But it would be wrong to portray him merely as the late heir of a proud tradition, for he was already feeling the first drafts of a new wind. He must not be called the poet of the end, as his poetry is ultimately based, not on the unstable values of civilization, but on nature and cosmic realities, and nature is forever changing.

In his most beautiful poems, Hesse is reconciled to the changes ordained by cosmic laws and watches them with serene equanimity. His hundreds of poems balance each other and in their entirety form an image of life which is centered on the golden rule. They did not need any laboriously worked out systematic arrangement and could be presented simply in chronological order.

Aside from the supervision of various editions of his work and the occasional writing of new poems and articles, Hesse's last years were taken up with the writing of answers to the many letters he received from friends and strangers alike. The flood of mail occasionally assumed massive proportions. Letters came from all social strata and all age groups and were often of a very personal character. Every one caused some emotional fatigue, and every answer strained the poet's limited strength. Yet he did not and would not hold back his helping hand where it could be of use. He knew that he could not solve his correspondents' problems, and could not send them a patent recipe, but he could share with them his faith in the meaning of life or at least in giving some meaning to it. His answers were sometimes blunt, and often uncomforting, but they were always sincere and never conventional. They were of course confidential and not meant for publication.

Occasionally, though, the confidence was broken, and thus his *Letter to Germany* of 1946 (*Ein Brief nach Deutschland,* VII, 445–453) was published in the Berlin *Neue Zeitung* against his wishes. It brought him a flood of insulting replies. He answered his critics in the *Neue Zürcher Zeitung.* Although many of his correspondents were of the opinion that one should not harass a deeply suffering nation with sermons, Hesse thought that the time of direst need and humiliation was also the best time for the necessary inner changes.

Hesse's reactions to the developments in Germany were widely shared by his fellow Swiss citizens, and their approval found public expression. In 1936 he received the Swiss Gottfried Keller Prize. In 1947 the University of Bern honored him with a Ph.D. degree, and on his eighty-fifth birthday Hesse became an honorary citizen of Montagnola. He voiced his gratitude in an acceptance speech delivered in Italian and spent the day with his intimates.

Hesse's last days were days without fear; days of melancholic serenity; days filled with patient waiting for the inevitable. In the summer of 1962 the poet's physician advised against the customary vacation trip to Sils Maria. He knew that the poet was suffering from leukemia, although to all appearances he was still enjoying good health.

On the morning of August 8 Hesse and his wife took a walk in the neighboring forest to gather dry wood for the fire. He stopped at a robinia with a rotting branch which he had often tried to tear loose, but it still would not come off. Somehow this branch became to him a symbol of a long lingering life and inspired him to verses:

> *Splittrig geknickter Ast,*
> *Hangend schon Jahr um Jahr,*
> *Trocken knarrt er im Wind sein Lied*
> *Ohne Laub, ohne Rinde,*
> *Kahl, fahl, zu langen Lebens,*
> *Zu langen Sterbens müd.*
> *Hart klingt und zäh sein Gesang,*

Klingt trotzig, klingt heimlich bang
Noch einen Sommer,
Noch einen Winter lang.

Branch, half splintered and bent,
Clinging year after year,
Drily you scrape your song in the wind,
Without bark, without foliage,
Bare, gray, and weary of
The long living, the long dying.
Harsh are your sounds and tough your song,
Spiteful it sounds and yet afraid,
Of another summer,
, And another winter.

Ninon Hesse remarked: "That is one of your most beautiful poems." Her husband smiled: "Then it is good."

When they came home, Hesse listened to a Mozart piano sonata, and his wife read to him, as on every evening. The following morning he died in his sleep from a brain hemorrhage.

Hesse was buried on the hot, bright afternoon of August 11 in the cemetery of S. Abbondio. His old friend, Deacon Völter, spoke at Hesse's grave. Other speakers were the Sindaco of Montagnola, Hesse's publisher, and other representatives from his German homeland. Finally Mendelssohn's canon *Beati Mortui* was sung: Blessed are they to whom death was granted in such a form!

Thomas Mann's death in 1955 preceded Hesse's by a few years. Some years later came the death of Rudolf Alexander Schröder and of Hesse's old friends, the painters Louis Moilliet and Ernst Morgenthaler. It was the end of an era.

Epilogue

The Modernity of Hesse

AT THE END of the nineteenth century, German culture still seemed secure to the average writer, and a rational view of the world appeared entirely demonstrable. However, the leading poets had already begun to question these assumptions. Young Gerhart Hauptmann, in spite of his so-called "naturalism," was treating the prophets of materialistic progress with irony, and young Thomas Mann in his *Buddenbrooks* evoked the image of a bourgeois society in decay.

Young Hermann Hesse also found the world of his parents highly questionable and attempted to withdraw from modern civilization into the timeless world of nature. He found himself unable to accept the conclusions of the materialists and felt more at home in the irrationalism of the older Romantic writers. Already he was convinced of the inadequacy of established Christianity and groping toward a deeper mysticism. He was uneasy about the prevailing social conditions and tried to overcome class differences by reviving the spirit of Franciscan brotherhood. The early writings of Hesse could be described as escapes from modern civilization into the small-town world of traditional German Romanticism.

Yet the shattering experience of World War I proved to Hesse that not even this village world was secure. Civilization could no longer be regenerated by playing one of its elements against the other. It was sick at its core. Not only modern man, but man as a whole, was a doubtful quantity, and the problem of civilization was not contemporary, but existential. Life had to be faced in its raw nakedness, and since all of its ugly external manifestations had their roots in man's soul, that soul had to be searched before any change could be initiated in the outside world. In *Demian*, Hesse began the descent into his own soul. In *Steppenwolf* he displayed its destructive ugliness as well as its healing powers. And in *Narcissus and Goldmund*, in *The Journey to the East*, and in *The Bead Game* he visualized the solution which allowed him to resume life once more and to take on its recurrent challenge in an attitude of faith.

In his turn inward, Hesse was aided by the older Romanticists. Novalis as well as Jean Paul had tried to lift the veil of nature and had experienced the totally contradictory character of human existence. But Hesse was encouraged by the changed climate of scientific research, although he never studied nuclear physics or the general theory of relativity.

Science in the second decade of the twentieth century had finally proved the assumptions of solid materialism to be untenable. The experiments of the researchers did not lead to absolute truth, but only to relative results dependent on the experimental conditions set up by the scientist. To paraphrase Werner Heisenberg, the popular differentiations between subjective and objective worlds, between Inward and Outward, between body and soul, are no longer fitting. The object of our research is not nature as such, but merely nature exposed to man. In his investigations of the so-called outside world, man is simply meeting himself. Hesse was right in quoting, at the beginning of his *Karamosoff* essay (VII, 161), Goethe's pronouncement that Inside and Outside are merely two terms for the same thing:

> Nichts ist drinnen, nichts ist draussen;
> Denn was innen, das ist aussen.

In addition, science had also abolished the nineteenth-century assumption of absolute time. Hesse had already stated in *Steppenwolf* that Albert Einstein had destroyed basic premises of occidental thought (IV, 266). He had demonstrated that all our time concepts are valid only for that sector of the physical world for which they are set up. It is entirely conceivable that different times exist side by side in the cosmos. When, therefore, Siddhartha experienced time as an illusion and the knight errants of *The Journey to the East* traveled in a time-space continuum, they merely expressed in poetic form what the scientists were saying by the formulas of mathematics.

It was no mere accident that mathematics played such an important part in *The Bead Game*. Had not already Novalis discovered that the life of the gods was revealed in mathematics? Had he not pronounced that all divine messengers must be mathematicians, and that mathematics was the main proof of the identity of nature with the human soul? Mathematics was also related to music, and music constituted a decisive part of Josef Knecht's education, especially the older music from Purcell to Mozart, which was built on mathematics and liberated mathematics from the rigidity of fixed formulas. In *The Journey to the East* King Solomon and Walther von der Vogelweide were just as present as Don Quixote and Novalis' Heinrich von Ofterdingen, and Lao-tse and Mozart were no longer separated by geographical boundaries. The world was paradoxical, and it was magical.

The new understanding of physical nature also demands a new interpretation of psychology. If external facts cannot be separated from the human observer in the physical sciences, then in psychology too the traditional separation of body and soul no longer is warranted. To differentiate between body and soul is of course useful and even necessary. But to differentiate is not to separate. In fact, the separation of body and soul became immediately suspect when Freud discovered the importance of the subconscious. It was no longer possible to consider psychological phenomena without their connection with the subconscious physical urges. But Freud and his early disciples hesitated to proceed further and still treated the human individual in a purely mechanical relation to his surroundings.

Modern psychology has gone back to the old Aristotelian concept of man as a social animal and considers the human personality within the social and historical spheres shaping it and in turn being shaped by it. And the most revolutionary representatives of psychology add even to this concept and take man's relation to transcendental realities as another necessary and inseparable extension of his total personality. Besides theological and philosophical disciples of Kierkegaard and Heidegger it was especially the Heidelberg psychologist Victor von Weizsäcker who developed this new, so-called "anthropological" concept of the human personality.*

It is surprising to see that Hesse's poetic vision of man anticipated this new psychological concept. He was duly thankful to Freud's psychoanalysis for opening his eyes to the importance of man's suppressed physical urges and never again overlooked the role of the animal parts in his make-up: man was directly connected with the nonhuman.

But Hesse also was too familiar with Romantic thought ever to forget the other side of man: his indissoluble connection with the superhuman. Already Peter Camenzind's and Knulp's quests were metaphysical. Thus, when Hesse became acquainted with psychoanalysis, even Jung's system appeared too individualistic to him, and he borrowed only isolated symbols from it. From *Demian* and *Siddhartha* on, man's relation to the infinite continued as a main concern of Hesse's works. They cannot be appreciated without being aware of his search for mystic unity.

Yet the mystic individual in Hesse's second period was isolated from its fellow human beings and looked at them with scorn and loathing. Now, a social concern was not foreign to Hesse and had already been displayed in his Gaienhofen stories and in his political essays. Thus when after *Steppenwolf* a calmer mood ushered in his third period, it came as no surprise that once more man was also interpreted as a social being. Man now had his roots in the social as well as the metaphysical sphere. In the end Hesse thus approached very closely the anthropological approach demanded by a truly up-to-date psychology.

Hesse's view of man can best be described as a poetic image of the total personality adumbrated by anthropological psychology. Here the individual stands in the spheres of nature and society just as much as he is indissolubly linked with history and with the forces of transcendency. Since we still largely

* Cf. Dieter Wyss. "Person und Begegnung in der Anthropologie Viktor von Weizsäckers," in: Arië Sborowitz and Ernst Michel, eds. *Der leidende Mensch. Personale Psychotherapie in anthropologischer Sicht* (Düsseldorf-Köln: Diederichs, 1960. Pp. 238–258).

connote scientific thinking with a strictly compartmental, rationalistic approach, Hesse's poetic vision for many contemporaries may provide an even better idea of modern psychological orientation than a strictly scientific description of it.

If thus the human world was paradoxical and magical, it was by no means unreal. Hesse from his beginnings rejected the interpretation of Nihilism, since he was deeply aware of the existence of an all-embracing divinity which could never be expressed in concrete anthropomorphic images, but was always accessible to mystic intuition. Its essence in fact defied the definitions of traditional theology. Hesse wholly rejected the oft-repeated tenets of Christianity and preferred the less familiar symbols of the Eastern religions. Here he could count on a receptive public that no longer believed, like previous generations, in the superiority of occidental technical civilization and its manifest destiny to rule the world.

As a result of the two world wars, European civilization has lost its central significance and has become merely one instrument in a global orchestra. World commerce and ever tightening international communications have brought the world together, and religions and cultures have intermingled to a hitherto unheard-of degree. Christianity has become one among many religions, it no longer leads them.

Hesse's religious position has been one of the significant symptoms of this development, and it has also materially helped in furthering it. We have seen that our poet has certainly not forsaken the spirit of Christian charity and has preserved the occidental attitude of active concern for the human world. But he has adopted the venerable images and parables of Eastern religions and has thus prepared the ground for the coming religion of humanity. Initially he was most attracted by the Franciscan interpretation of Christianity. Later, a decided turn toward Vedantic philosophy could be discerned. In the end Hesse discovered the closest correspondence to his own point of view in Chinese Universism.

Yet in whatever form he set down his metaphysical convictions, he never wrote in the abstract terms of rational philosophy. His was the more suggestive language of art, which need not fear the paradox and the magical. From *Demian* on, Hesse's style can no longer be called Impressionistic or, in spite of its antecedents, Romantic. It is taking the world seriously, but not too seriously. For the world of Hesse's novels has no existence outside of the writer's soul; he can change it at will and use its symbols at will. To be sure, Hesse is no nihilist like Sartre. The real world of everyday life is there, just as it was there for Jean Paul.

This older writer shunned contact with the ordinary world around him as little as did Hesse. In the midst of his sentimental Romantic flights, Jean Paul devised the figure of the aeronaut Gianozzo who saw the world from above, and saw in it not only flower gardens and alpine meadows, but also bristling fortresses and gory battlegrounds. At the turn of the eighteenth century Jean Paul visualized bursting metropolitan centers, aerial navies, an American conquest of Europe, and an exploration of the moon.

In the same way the mature Hesse did not want to oppose civilization with a bucolic world. His Knulp was not an ideal figure drawn with sugary sweetness. And already in those years when the poet seemed closest to nature, he undertook a Zeppelin trip (in 1910) and viewed the Swiss landscape from an airplane (in 1912).

He was also the most pronounced critic af all reactionary political systems founded on Romanticism. Already the early Hesse poked fun at vegetarianism and criticized the German student fraternities of the *Altheidelberg* ("The Student Prince") variety with their flags, their ribbons, and their uniforms. He was a contributor to liberal periodicals. Hesse's decided turn against the German nationalism of 1914 was anything but romantic. In later years he never succumbed, like Benn, to the temptation to see a progressive way to a new culture in the mythology and pseudo-biology of Nazism.

Yet Hesse nowhere portrayed the modern world seriously. When he liked it, he liked it as a game and as a pleasant illusion. Its vaunted order was artificial. He knew the dangers of abstract intellectualism and showed them up in Master Tegularius of *The Bead Game*. As much as he admired the spiritual discipline and order in the philosophy of the Chinese *I Ching* and the regulated life of the Benedictine monasteries, he knew that they did not represent ultimate truth.

In the end, Josef Knecht left the well regulated world of the Bead Game and looked for an inner, non-objective world. This world was Romantic only in the sense in which another modern, the painter Paul Klee, spoke of the "cool romanticism" of his pictures. When Hesse in his *Trip to Nuremberg* visualized the reversion of a civilized city to weasel and marten, he paralled modern painting's suggestion of a primeval landscape following the catastrophe of civilization. It was there, in a primeval world no longer man-made, that man could come to grips with the problem of his existence.

In the final analysis this problem was very simple, and therefore could be described without stylistic involutions. If anything demonstrates Hesse's unromantic sobriety, it is his style. It is a clear and concise style, admirably fitting into the German tradition and at the same time akin to Chinese simplicity. It has for its ancestors the style of the Grimm brothers, of Wackenroder and Novalis, of Luther. And it resulted not from childish drifting, but from mature concentration. Hesse, like so many modern writers, could have abandoned himself. To be sure, he occasionally tried his hand at surrealistic mannerisms, though he never seriously adopted them. The exuberance of *Klingsor's Last Summer* remained a mere episode.

It also must not be forgotten that the novels written after *Klingsor* by no means refrain from richness and variety. The style of *Siddhartha* captivates by its linear purity and its delicate musicality, while *The Trip to Nuremberg* is ironical, and the style of *Steppenwolf* deeply contrapuntal. *Narcissus and Goldmund* appeals as a straight narrative, but one built over a contest between two worlds, in which rich pictures of reality contrast with philosophical passages of great depth. *The Journey to the East* develops the same conflict as a stylistic contest between involved sentences tending to abstraction and concrete clauses of visual strength. Finally, *The Bead Game* moves between an esoteric world of spiritual ritual and a transparent realm of sunlit mountain scenery and youthful exuberance. To call Hesse's style pale or even weak is wilful detraction. The most simple descriptions in *The Journey to the East* and *The Bead Game* are also the richest in overtones.

The clarity of Hesse's language was meant as a defense against chaos. Its simplicity is frequently misunderstood. André Gide saw more deeply:

> With Hesse not the emotion or the thought is subdued, but only the expression; and it is kept back by the rare feeling for decency and control, for harmony and for the mutual cosmic dependence of things. I believe that only very few Germans are capable of this latent irony, the absolute absence of which disturbs me in the works of many German authors who are taking themselves so dreadfully seriously" (Introduction to the French translation of *The Journey to the East*).

Thomas Mann also understood Hesse's use of distance and irony to describe German depth. He saw that here was a manly individual protesting against the chaotic turn toward war and revolution and the self-deception of bourgeois sentimentalism. Hesse hated the clamor for a "leader," since it presupposed a lack of responsibility and a fear of independent thought. He rejected not only Hitler, but any kind of a Führer. He was a stubborn nonconformist. In retrospect Hesse could call all his works from *Peter Camenzind* on "a defense [and at times also a call for help] of the personality and the individual" (*Briefe*. Enlarged edition, 1964, p. 418).

This individualism also made Hesse shun literary cliques and avoid literary classification as much as possible. In *The Trip to Nuremberg* he expressed his belief that the last great period of German literature had ended about 1850 and that it was impossible to continue its forms (IV, 156). His own generation, he felt, should not aim at beauty, but at sincerity, although it had not yet found an adequate expression for it. Nietzsche's *Ecce homo* and other exceptional books showed only the lack of direction. And psychoanalysis which indicated a partial progress, became bogged down in a harness of dogmatic vanity (IV, 157).

It was dangerous to replace the needed direction by propaganda. The disturbing growth of petty literary cliques, of journalistic conspiracies, of literary promotions, has frequently marred the modern literary scene. But artificial syntheses in the end will not prevail, and it is safer to consider the field of modern culture for what it is: a field of ruins and widely scattered new growths, among which a few may contain the germs of a new culture. If one seeks a common denominator for all the individual attempts, one must call the new style dissociative, inasmuch as it dissociates itself from the old tradition and dissolves its structures into their various elements. And one can perhaps also call it surrealistic, as it tries to find new, meaningful connections of these elements, which in any case are different from those of traditional reality.

It is into this general background that Hesse's works since *Demian* fit surprisingly well. They fit in their dissociation from traditional reality and their attempt to find a new style transcending it. They also fit in their pronounced individualism. It is almost mandatory to consider Hesse's works in an individualistic aspect. But it happens that his individualism is representative and responsible. Figures like Josef Knecht can guide us into a more harmonious and mutually considerate civilization. New ages have always started from within.

SELECTED BIBLIOGRAPHY

BIBLIOGRAPHIES:

Mileck, Joseph. *Hermann Hesse and His Critics. The Criticism and Bibliography of Half a Century.* (University of North Carolina Studies in Germanic Languages and Literatures, No. 21.) Chapel Hill, N.C.: University of North Carolina Press, 1958.

Waibler, Helmut. *Hermann Hesse. Eine Bibliographie.* Bern: Francke, 1962.

WORKS OF HERMANN HESSE:

IN GERMAN:

Briefe. Enlarged edition. (Die Bücher der Neunzehn, No. 117.) Frankfurt am Main: Suhrkamp, 1964.

Gesammelte Schriften. 7 vols. Berlin: Suhrkamp, 1957.

Zum Gedächtnis unseres Vaters. (In collaboration with Adele Hesse.) Tübingen: Wunderlich, 1930.

IN TRANSLATION:

"In the Fog," in *A Harvest of German Verse.* Tr. Margarete Münsterberg. New York. 1917.

In Sight of Chaos (Blick ins Chaos). Tr. Stephen Hudson. Zürich: Verlag Seldwyla, 1923.

Steppenwolf. Tr. Basil Creighton. London: Secker, 1929.

Death and the Lover (Narziss und Goldmund). Tr. Geoffrey Dunlop. New York: Mead and Co., 1932; London: Jarrold, 1932; Reprinted as *Goldmund.* London: Owen, Vision Press, 1959.

"A Life in Brief" (Kurzgefasster Lebenslauf). Tr. Mervyn Savill. *Horizon* (1946), 175–190.

Le voyage en Orient (Die Morgenlandfahrt). Préface de André Gide. Paris: Calmann-Lévy, 1948.

Demian. With a Foreword by Thomas Mann. Tr. N. H. Friday. New York: Holt, 1948.

Magister Ludi (Das Glasperlenspiel). Tr. Mervyn Savill. London: Aldus, 1949; New York: Holt, 1949; Reprint: New York: Frederick Ungar, 1957.

Siddhartha. Tr. Hilda Rosner. New York: New Directions, 1951; London: Owen, Vision Press, 1955.

Gertrude. Tr. Hilda Rosner. London: Owen, Vision Press, 1955.

The Journey to the East. Tr. Hilda Rosner. London: Owen, Vision Press, 1956; New York: Noonday Press, 1957.

The Prodigy (Unterm Rad). Tr. Walter J. Strachan. London: Owen, Vision Press, 1958.

Demian. Tr. Walter J. Strachan. London: Owen, Vision Press, 1958.

Peter Camenzind. Tr. Walter J. Strachan. London: Owen, Vision Press, 1961.

Steppenwolf. Tr. Basil Creighton. Revised by Joseph Mileck and Horst Frenz. New York: Holt, Rinehart, and Winston, 1963.

SPECIAL LITERATURE ON HESSE:

Ball, Hugo. *Hermann Hesse. Sein Leben und sein Werk.* Fortgeführt von Anni Carlsson und Otto Basler. Zürich: Fretz & Wasmuth, 1947.

Baumler, Franz. *Hermann Hesse.* (Köpfe des XX. Jahrhunderts, Nr. 10.) Berlin: Colloqium Verlag, 1959.

Carlsson, Anni. *Hermann Hesses Gedichte.* Zürich: Fretz & Wasmuth, 1943.

Cohn, Hilde, D. "The Symbolic End of Hermann Hesse's 'Glasperlenspiel,'" *Modern Language Quarterly,* XI (1950), 347–357.

Farquharson, R. H. "The Identity and Significance of Leo in Hesse's 'Morgenlandfahrt,'" *Monatshefte* (University of Wisconsin), LV (1963), 122–128.

Fickert, Kurt J. *The Problem of the Artist and the Philistine in the Work of Hermann Hesse*. Unpublished Ph. D. dissertation, New York University, 1952.

———. "The Development of the Outsider Concept in Hesse's Novels," *Monatshefte*, LII (1960), 171–178.

Field, G. Wallis. "Hermann Hesse as Critic of English and American Literature," *Monatshefte*, LIII (1961), 147–158.

Flaxman, Seymour L. "Der Steppenwolf. Hesse's Portrait of the Intellectual," *Modern Language Quarterly*, XV (1954), 349–358.

Freedman, Ralph. "Romantic Imagination. Hermann Hesse as a Modern Novelist," *PMLA*, LXXIII (1958), 275–289.

Hafner, Gotthilf. "Das letzte Gedicht. Zum Gedenken an Hermann Hesse," *Welt und Wort*, XVIII (1963), 78.

Halpert, Inge D. "Vita Activa and Vita Contemplativa," *Monatshefte*, LIII (1961), 159–166.

Heller, Peter. "The Creative Unconscious and the Spirit. A Study of Polarities in Hesse's Image of the Writer," *Modern Language Forum*, XXXVIII (1953), 28–40.

———. "The Writer in Conflict with His Age. A Study in the Ideology of Hermann Hesse," *Monatshefte*, XLVI (1954), 137–147.

Hill, Claude. "Hermann Hesse and Germany," *German Quarterly*, XXI (1948), 9–15.

———. "Hermann Hesse als Kritiker der bürgerlichen Zivilisation," *Monatshefte*, XL (1948), 241–253.

Maier, Emanuel. *The Psychology of C. G. Jung in the Works of Hermann Hesse*. Unpublished Ph. D. dissertation, New York University, 1952.

Mayer, Gerhart. *Die Begegnung des Christentums mit den asiatischen Religionen im Werk Hermann Hesses*. (Untersuchungen zur allgemeinen Religionsgeschichte, N. S. Nr. 1.) Bonn: Röhrscheid, 1956.

Middleton, J. C. "Hermann Hesse's 'Morgenlandfahrt,'" *Germanic Review*, XXXII (1957), 299–310.

Mileck, Joseph. "Hermann Hesse's 'Glasperlenspiel,'" *University of California Publications in Modern Philology*, XXXVI (1952), 245–270.

————. "Names and the Creative Process," *Monatshefte*, LIII (1961), 167–180.

Negus, Kenneth. "On the Death of Josef Knecht in Hermann Hesse's 'Glasperlenspiel,' " *Monatshefte*, LIII (1961), 181–189.

Schmid, Max. *Hermann Hesse. Weg und Wandlung.* Mit einem bibliographischen Anhang von Arnim Lemp. Zürich: Fretz & Wasmuth, 1947; English: *Hermann Hesse. Growth of a Poet.* Tr. A. A. Dawson. Unpublished M. A. dissertation, Southern Methodist University, 1949.

Schwarz, Egon. "Zur Erklärung von Hesse's 'Steppenwolf,' " *Monatshefte*, LIII (1961), 191–198.

Shaw, Leroy R. "Time and the Structure of Hermann Hesse's 'Siddhartha,' " *Symposium*, XI (1957), 204–224.

Willecke, Frederick H(enry). *The Style and Form of Hermann Hesse's Gaienhofer Novellen.* Unpublished Ph. D. dissertation, New York University, 1960.

————. "Style and Form of Hermann Hesse's 'Unterm Rad,' " *Kentucky Foreign Language Quarterly*, VIII (1961), 147–156.

Willson, A. Leslie, "Hesse's Veil of Isis," *Monatshefte*, LV (1963), 313–321.

Zeller, Bernhard. *Hermann Hesse. Eine Chronik in Bildern.* Bearbeitet und mit einer Einführung versehen. Frankfurt am Main: Suhrkamp, 1960; New edition: *Hermann Hesse in Selbstzeugnissen und Bilddokumenten.* (Rowohlts Monographien, Nr. 85.) Reinbek bei Hamburg: Rowohlt, 1963.

Zimmermann, Werner. "Hermann Hesse, Morgenlandfahrt," in his *Deutsche Prosadichtungen der Gegenwart*, I (Düsseldorf: Schwann. 4. ed. 1962), 229–249.

Ziolkowski, Theodore. *Hermann Hesse und Novalis.* Unpublished Ph. D. dissertation, Yale University, 1956.

————. "Hermann Hesse's 'Steppenwolf.' A Sonata in Prose," *Modern Language Quarterly*, XIX (1958), 115–133.

————. "Hesse's Chiliastic Vision," *Monatshefte*, LIII (1961), 199–210.

INDEX OF NAMES AND TITLES

Hesse's prose works are listed under their English as well as their German titles. The first adjective or noun of the title determines the alphabetical arrangement.